Expert T-SQL Window Functions in SQL Server 2019

The Hidden Secret to Fast Analytic and Reporting Queries

Second Edition

Kathi Kellenberger
Clayton Groom
Ed Pollack

Apress®

Expert T-SQL Window Functions in SQL Server 2019

Kathi Kellenberger
Edwardsville, IL, USA

Clayton Groom
Smithton, IL, USA

Ed Pollack
Albany, NY, USA

ISBN-13 (pbk): 978-1-4842-5196-6
https://doi.org/10.1007/978-1-4842-5197-3

ISBN-13 (electronic): 978-1-4842-5197-3

Managing Director, Apress Media LLC: Welmoed Spahr
Acquisitions Editor: Jonathan Gennick
Development Editor: Laura Berendson
Coordinating Editor: Jill Balzano

Cover image designed by Freepik (www.freepik.com)

Distributed to the book trade worldwide by Springer Science+Business Media New York, 233 Spring Street, 6th Floor, New York, NY 10013. Phone 1-800-SPRINGER, fax (201) 348-4505, e-mail orders-ny@springer-sbm.com, or visit www.springeronline.com. Apress Media, LLC is a California LLC and the sole member (owner) is Springer Science + Business Media Finance Inc (SSBM Finance Inc). SSBM Finance Inc is a **Delaware** corporation.

For information on translations, please e-mail rights@apress.com, or visit http://www.apress.com/rights-permissions.

Apress titles may be purchased in bulk for academic, corporate, or promotional use. eBook versions and licenses are also available for most titles. For more information, reference our Print and eBook Bulk Sales web page at http://www.apress.com/bulk-sales.

Any source code or other supplementary material referenced by the author in this book is available to readers on GitHub via the book's product page, located at www.apress.com/9781484251966. For more detailed information, please visit http://www.apress.com/source-code.

Printed on acid-free paper

This book is dedicated to the memory of Larry Toothman.

Table of Contents

About the Authors

Kathi Kellenberger is a data platform MVP and the editor of Simple Talk at Redgate Software. She has worked with SQL Server for over 20 years. She is also coleader of the PASS Women in Technology Virtual Group and an instructor at LaunchCode. In her spare time, Kathi enjoys spending time with family and friends, singing, and cycling.

Clayton Groom is a data warehouse and analytics consultant at Clayton Groom, LLC. He has worked with SQL Server for 25 years. His expertise lies in designing and building data warehouse and analytic solutions on the Microsoft technology stack, including Power BI, SQL Server, Analysis Services, Reporting Services, and Excel.

Ed Pollack has over 20 years of experience in database and systems administration and architecture, developing a passion for performance optimization and making things go faster. He has spoken at many SQL Saturdays, 24 Hours of PASS, and PASS Summits and has coordinated SQL Saturday Albany since its inception in 2014.

About the Technical Reviewer

 **Rodney Landrum** went to school to be a poet and a writer. And then he graduated, so that dream was crushed. He followed another path, which was to become a professional in the fun-filled world of information technology. He has worked as a systems engineer, UNIX and network admin, data analyst, client services director, and finally as a database administrator. The old hankering to put words on paper, while paper still existed, got the best of him, and in 2000 he began writing technical articles, some creative and humorous, some quite the opposite. In 2010, he wrote *SQL Server Tacklebox*, a title his editor disdained, but a book closest to the true creative potential he sought; he still yearned to do a full book without a single screenshot, which he accomplished in 2019 with his first novel, *Chronicles of Shameus*. He currently works from his castle office in Pensacola, FL, as a senior DBA consultant for Ntirety, a division of Hostway/HOSTING.

Foreword

SQL was developed in the 1970s and became standardized through ANSI-approved committees as a formal standard starting in 1986.[1] Today in 2019, SQL has become the most widely used declarative language. Along the way, window functions have come to be an important part of that standard. ANSI does not make standards but plays an important role in documenting and preserving them. The individual software vendors voluntarily decide to comply, and it's the work of the authors of books like this one to explain SQL use in practical terms.

In my own career in data science and advanced analytics, window functions have been an important part of several key projects in the past few years. Several years ago, I made a YouTube video for a user group based on the earlier edition of this book. Since then, as a career architect at Microsoft, I have advised the application for data science. In one project, the input of about 20 features was not yielding adequate results: using window functions, a team under my leadership (and yes, direct coding) quickly grew that number to over 1,000. More than numeric growth, the accuracy rates improved, and on the business story, the organization is saving millions of dollars annually for their question. In the past month, I have encountered an unrelated new project, and a similar story is there: a time-series type of data set and an opportunity to grow from under 20 features to a number much larger.

One wonders whether automated machine learning technologies would make such combinations on their own, and I'm skeptical. Making a robust set of features from window functions requires not just time-series considerations but also clustering knowledge based on knowing the data domain. Even if automated technologies make great progress in this topic, I anticipate the need for any data scientist to have simple knowledge of these functions for the more typical data science investigation which has only a few features and low number of observations.

SQL is central to on-premise and cloud database technologies – and in the data science world, many use Apache Spark (part of SQL Server 2019 and so many other data technologies). This reach into advanced analytics is yet another reason why this topic is

---

[1]See https://blog.ansi.org/2018/10/sql-standard-iso-iec-9075-2016-ansi-x3-135/

an expert-level subject in the SQL language. The mainstream applications extend from any business analytics SQL query and even into supporting advanced analytics and machine learning algorithms.

Over the years, it's been an honor to individually know Kathi Kellenberger and Clayton Groom as respected peers and professionals and to see how they have each become important leaders to the technical user community through many presentations (for which they typically volunteer their own time) and through the creation and now revision of this book. In this revision, Ed Pollack has applied material on baseball statistics, illustrating that not every time series is about money. It's not enough to have a standard written, but one needs to have expert coaches to explain how these functions describe an approach for business analytics. This book has rich examples and altogether provides a clear path into one of the most mathematically complex and yet practically useful aspects of the SQL language.

Mark Tabladillo, Ph.D.
Cloud Solution Architect, Microsoft

Acknowledgments

The first edition of this book would not have been written except for the suggestion of one of my friends in the data platform community, Larry Toothman. Sadly, Larry passed away shortly after the book was published and before I could get a copy to him. Larry was just getting started with presenting at events and being more involved in the community during the last couple of years of his life. Who knows what he might have accomplished if things had turned out differently. Thanks to Larry's inspiration, people around the world will learn about windowing functions.

They say it takes a village to raise a child, and the same might be true for a book. I would like to thank Jonathan Gennick and Jill Balzano for their help and guidance. There are probably many people at Apress who had a hand in this project that I'll never meet, and I would like to thank them as well.

Clayton Groom and Ed Pollack each wrote about their real-world experience using windowing functions. In each case, the idea for their chapter came from my running into each of them at user group meetings and just talking about my project. Their contributions definitely make this a better and more enjoyable book for you.

Thanks to Rodney Landrum for doing a great job on the technical review and to Mark Tabladillo for the wonderful foreword.

Thank you to my family, especially my husband, Dennis, who takes care of just about everything around the house. He makes my life so much easier when I take on big projects like this.

Finally, thank you dear reader for learning about windowing functions from this book. I hope that you enjoy it and can apply the things you learn right away. I would love to hear from you at events, so don't be shy!

Introduction

Several years ago, I would create a user group presentation for each new version of SQL Server about the new T-SQL features. There was so much to say in 2012 that I decided to build a presentation on just the windowing functions introduced that year. Eventually, I had so much material that it turned into two sessions. Over the years, I have probably presented this information at least 50 times at events around the United States and the United Kingdom. Despite that, most people still are not using windowing functions because they haven't heard about them or do not realize the benefits.

What's in This Book?

This book covers each type of windowing function beginning with the ranking functions introduced with SQL Server 2005 through the statistical functions introduced in 2012. Each chapter explains how to use the functions along with any options and provides a few simple examples of how to use them. Unfortunately, the last time that Microsoft added any new windowing functions was 2012, but there have been some performance improvements more recently. One chapter is dedicated to the performance of windowing functions.

Finally, the last two chapters in the book cover some real-world examples. In Chapter 9, you'll learn how to analyze a large data set, over 100 years of baseball statistics. Chapters 10 and 11 show how windowing functions can be used in data warehouse calculations instead of building a cube.

Intended Audience

This book is meant for people who already have good T-SQL skills. They know how to join tables, use subqueries and CTEs, and write aggregate queries. Despite these skills, they occasionally run into problems that are not easy to solve in a set-based manner. Without windowing functions, some of these problems can only be solved by using cursors or expensive triangular joins. By using the concepts taught in this book, your T-SQL skills will improve to the next level. Once you start using windowing functions, you'll find even more reasons to learn them.

Contacting the Author

Great care was taken to ensure that the information presented is correct, but sometimes readers come up with a better way to write a query or find an error. You can contact me at kathi.kellenberger@outlook.com with any comments or questions.

CHAPTER 1

Looking Through the Window

SQL Server is a powerful database platform with a versatile query language called T-SQL. The most exciting T-SQL enhancement over the years, in my opinion, is the window functions. Window functions enable you to solve query problems in new, easier ways and with better performance most of the time over traditional techniques. They are a great tool for analytics. You may hear these called "windowing" or "windowed" functions as well. The three terms are synonymous when talking about this feature.

After the release of SQL Server 2000, SQL Server enthusiasts waited 5 long years for the next version of SQL Server to arrive. Microsoft delivered an entirely new product with SQL Server 2005. This version brought SQL Server Management Studio, SQL Server Integration Services, snapshot isolation, and database mirroring. Microsoft also enhanced T-SQL with many great features, such as common table expressions (CTEs). The most exciting T-SQL enhancement of all with 2005 was the introduction of window functions.

That was just the beginning. Window functions are part of the standard ANSI SQL specification beginning with ANSI SQL2003. More functionality according to the standard was released with version 2012 of SQL Server. In 2019, Microsoft gave some of the window functions a performance boost with batch mode processing, a feature once reserved for column store indexes. You'll see how this performance feature works in Chapter 8. Even now, the functionality falls short of the entire specification, so there is more to look forward to in the future.

This chapter provides a first look at two T-SQL window functions, LAG and ROW_NUMBER. You will learn just what the window is and how to define it with the OVER clause. You will also learn how to divide the windows into smaller sections called partitions.

© Kathi Kellenberger, Clayton Groom, and Ed Pollack 2019
K. Kellenberger et al., *Expert T-SQL Window Functions in SQL Server 2019*,
https://doi.org/10.1007/978-1-4842-5197-3_1

Discovering Window Functions

Window functions do not let you do anything that was impossible to do with earlier functionality, and they have nothing to do with the Microsoft Windows API. Using previously available methods, such as self-joins, correlated subqueries, and cursors, you can solve just about any T-SQL problem if you work at it long and hard enough. The main benefit of window functions is the ease with which you can solve these tricky queries. Most of the time, you also realize a big boost in performance over the older methods. You can often use a window function to change a solution involving many statements or subqueries to one easier statement.

I like to divide window functions into several categories that do not exactly match up with the way Microsoft defines them: ranking functions, window aggregates, accumulating window aggregates, offset functions, and statistical functions. (Microsoft refers to the four offset and four statistical functions as "analytic" functions.) You can use these functions to assign a rank to each row, calculate summary values without grouping, calculate running totals, include columns from different rows in your results, and calculate percentages over a group. You'll learn about these functions as you read this book.

My favorite T-SQL function which also happens to be a window function is called LAG. It is one of the offset functions, which you will learn about in Chapter 6. LAG allows you to include columns from different rows in your results. Using LAG is easier and performs better than older methods that do the same thing.

Within the same year (just a few months apart), two different people approached me for help with essentially the same problem: using data from the stock market, how can one compare the closing price of a stock from one day to the next? The traditional solution requires that each row of the data be joined to the prior row to get the closing price from the previous day. By using the LAG function, the solution is not only simpler to write, it also performs much better.

Note   If you would like to follow along with this example, a sample script to create the StockAnalysisDemo database and generated stock market data can be found along with the code for this chapter on the Apress site.

For a quick look at how to solve this problem first by using one of the traditional methods and then by using LAG, review and run Listing 1-1.

Listing 1-1. Two Approaches to Solving the Stock Market Problem

```
USE StockAnalysisDemo;
GO
--1-1.1 Using a subquery
SELECT TickerSymbol, TradeDate, ClosePrice,
    (SELECT TOP(1) ClosePrice
    FROM StockHistory AS SQ
    WHERE SQ.TickerSymbol  = OQ.TickerSymbol
        AND SQ.TradeDate < OQ.TradeDate
    ORDER BY TradeDate DESC) AS PrevClosePrice
FROM StockHistory AS OQ
ORDER BY TickerSymbol, TradeDate;

--1-1.2 Using LAG
SELECT TickerSymbol, TradeDate, ClosePrice,
    LAG(ClosePrice) OVER(PARTITION BY TickerSymbol
            ORDER BY TradeDate) AS PrevClosePrice
FROM StockHistory
ORDER BY TickerSymbol, TradeDate;
```

The partial results are shown in Figure 1-1. Since the data is randomly generated, the values of ClosePrice and PrevClosePrice in the image will not match your values. Query 1 uses a correlated subquery, the old method, to select one ClosePrice for every outer row. By joining the TickerSymbol from the inner query to the outer query you ensure that you are not comparing two different stocks. The inner and outer queries are also joined by the TradeDate, but the TradeDate for the inner query must be less than the outer query to make sure you get the prior day. The inner query must also be sorted to get the row that has the latest data but still less than the current date. This query took over a minute to run on my laptop, which has 16GB of RAM and is using SSD storage. Almost 700,000 rows were returned.

Query 2 uses the window function LAG to solve the same problem and produces the same results. Don't worry about the syntax at this point; you will be an expert by the end of this book. The query using LAG took just 13 seconds to run on my laptop.

	TickerSymbol	TradeDate	ClosePrice	PrevClosePrice
1	Z1	2017-01-03	26.98	NULL
2	Z1	2017-01-04	27.94	26.98
3	Z1	2017-01-05	27.89	27.94
4	Z1	2017-01-06	28.44	27.89
5	Z1	2017-01-09	28.87	28.44
	TickerSymbol	TradeDate	ClosePrice	PrevClosePrice
1	Z1	2017-01-03	26.98	NULL
2	Z1	2017-01-04	27.94	26.98
3	Z1	2017-01-05	27.89	27.94
4	Z1	2017-01-06	28.44	27.89
5	Z1	2017-01-09	28.87	28.44

Figure 1-1. *Partial results of the stock market problem*

By just looking at the code in Listing 1-1, you can see that Query 2 using LAG is much simpler to write, even though you may not understand the syntax just yet. It also runs much faster because it is just reading the table once instead of once per row like Query 1. As you continue reading this book and running the examples, you will learn how window functions like LAG will make your life easier and your customers happier!

Thinking About the Window

Window functions are different than regular functions because they operate over a set of rows, also called a *window*. This may sound similar to how aggregate functions work. Aggregate functions, such as SUM and AVG, operate on groups of rows and provide summary values. When you write an aggregate query, you lose the detail columns except for those in the GROUP BY clause.

When adding a GROUP BY clause, instead of returning a summary along with all the rows, you will see a summary row, one row for each unique set of GROUP BY columns. For example, to get a count of the all the rows using an aggregate query, you must leave out the other columns. Once you add columns into the SELECT and GROUP BY, you get a count for each unique grouping, not the entire set of results.

Queries with window functions are much different than traditional aggregate queries. There are no restrictions to the columns that appear in the SELECT list, and no GROUP BY clause is required. You can also add window functions to aggregate queries, and that will be discussed in Chapter 3. Instead of summary rows being returned, all the details are returned and the result of the expression with the window function is included as just another column. In fact, by using a window function to get the overall count of the rows, you could still include all of the columns in the table.

Imagine looking through a window to see a specific set of rows while your query is running. You have one last chance to perform an operation, such as grabbing one of the columns from another row. The result of the operation is added as an additional column. You will learn how window functions really work as you read this book, but the idea of looking through the window has helped me understand and explain window functions to audiences at many SQL Server events. Figure 1-2 illustrates this concept.

	TickerSymbol	TradeDate	ClosePrice	PrevClosePrice
1	Z1	2017-01-03	26.98	NULL
2	Z1	2017-01-04	27.94	26.98
3	Z1	2017-01-05	27.89	27.94
4	Z1	2017-01-06	28.44	27.89
5	Z1	2017-01-09	28.87	28.44

The Window

TickerSymbol	TradeDate	ClosePrice	OpenPrice
Z1	2017-01-04	27.94	28.44
Z1	2017-01-05	27.89	28.39

Figure 1-2. Looking through the window to perform an operation on a set of rows

The window is not limited to the columns found in the SELECT list of the query. For example, if you take a look at the StockHistory table, you will see that there is also an OpenPrice column. The OpenPrice from one day is not the same as the ClosePrice from the previous day. If you wanted to, you could use LAG to include the previous OpenPrice in the results even though it is not included in the SELECT list originally.

In the stock history example using LAG, each row has its own window where it finds the previous close price. When the calculation is performed on the third row of the data, the window consists of the second and third rows. When the calculation is performed on the fourth row, the window consists of the third and fourth rows.

What would happen if the rows for 2017-12-02 were removed from the query by a WHERE clause? Does the window contain filtered-out rows? The answer is "No," which brings up two very important concepts to understand when using window functions: where window functions may be used in the query and the logical order of operations.

Window functions may only be used in the SELECT list and ORDER BY clause. You cannot filter or group on window functions. In situations where you must filter or group on the results of a window function, the solution is to separate the logic. You could use a temp table, derived table subquery, or a CTE and then filter or group in the outer query.

Window functions operate after the FROM, WHERE, GROUP BY, and HAVING clauses. They operate before the TOP and DISTINCT clauses are evaluated. You will learn more about how DISTINCT and TOP affect queries with window functions in the "Uncovering Special Case Windows" section later in this chapter.

The window is defined by the OVER clause. Notice in Query 2 of Listing 1-1 that the LAG function is followed by an OVER clause. Each type of window function has specific requirements for the OVER clause. The LAG function must have an ORDER BY expression and may have a PARTITION BY expression.

Understanding the OVER Clause

One thing that sets window functions apart is the OVER clause, which defines the window or set. With one exception I'll explain in Chapter 7, window functions will have an OVER clause, and learning how to use the OVER clause is required to understand window functions. In some cases, the OVER clause will be empty. You will see empty OVER clauses in Chapter 3 when working with window aggregate functions.

Note   There is one situation in which you will see the OVER keyword in a query not following a window function, and that is with the sequence object. The sequence object, introduced with SQL Server 2008, is a bucket containing incrementing numbers often used in place of an identity column.

For any type of expression in the SELECT list of a query, a calculation is performed for each row in the results. For example, if you had a query with the expression Col1 + Col2, those two columns would be added together once for every row returned. A calculation is performed for row 1, row 2, row 3, and so on. Expressions with window functions must also be calculated once per row. In this case, however, the expressions operate over a set of rows that can be different for each row where the calculation is performed.

The OVER clause determines which rows make up the window. The OVER clause has three possible components: PARTITION BY, ORDER BY, and the frame. The PARTITION BY expression divides up the rows, and it's optional depending on what you are trying to accomplish. The ORDER BY expression is required for some types of window functions.

Where it is used, it determines the order in which the window function is applied. Finally, the frame is used for some specific types of window functions to provide even more granularity. You'll learn about framing in Chapter 5.

Many T-SQL developers and database professionals have used the ROW_NUMBER function. They may not have even realized that this is one of the window functions. There are many situations where adding a row number to the query is a step along the way to solving a complex query problem.

ROW_NUMBER supplies an incrementing number, starting with one, for each row. The order in which the numbers are applied is determined by the columns specified in the ORDER BY expression, which is independent of an ORDER BY clause found in the query itself. Run the queries in Listing 1-2 to see how this works.

Listing 1-2. Applying the Row Numbers to Different Columns

```
USE AdventureWorks;
GO
--1-2.1 Row numbers applied by CustomerID
SELECT CustomerID, SalesOrderID,
    ROW_NUMBER() OVER(ORDER BY CustomerID) AS RowNumber
FROM Sales.SalesOrderHeader;

--1-2.2 Row numbers applied by SalesOrderID
SELECT CustomerID, SalesOrderID,
    ROW_NUMBER() OVER(ORDER BY SalesOrderID) AS RowNumber
FROM Sales.SalesOrderHeader;
```

Note   The AdventureWorks and AdventureWorksDW databases are used in many of the examples throughout this book. You can use any version starting with 2014 or later to follow along, and the 2017 version was the latest available at the time of this writing. Just be sure to adjust the USE statement when it's included to fit your version of the databases.

The OVER clause follows the ROW_NUMBER function. Inside the OVER clause, you will see ORDER BY followed by one or more columns. The difference between Queries 1 and 2 is just the ORDER BY expression within the OVER clause. Notice in the partial results shown in Figure 1-3 that the row numbers end up applied in the order of the column found in the ORDER BY expression of the OVER clause, which is also the order that the data is returned. Since the data must be sorted to apply the row numbers, it is easy for the data to stay in that order, but it is not guaranteed. The only way to ever actually guarantee the order of the results is to add an ORDER BY to the query.

	CustomerID	SalesOrderID	RowNumber
1	11000	43793	1
2	11000	51522	2
3	11000	57418	3
4	11001	43767	4
5	11001	51493	5
6	11001	72773	6

	CustomerID	SalesOrderID	RowNumber
1	29825	43659	1
2	29672	43660	2
3	29734	43661	3
4	29994	43662	4
5	29565	43663	5
6	29898	43664	6

Figure 1-3. *Partial results of using ROW_NUMBER with different OVER clauses*

If the query itself has an ORDER BY clause, it can be different than the ORDER BY within OVER. Listing 1-3 demonstrates this.

Listing 1-3. Using ROW_NUMBER with a Different ORDER BY in the OVER Clause

```
--1-3.1 Row number with a different ORDER BY
SELECT CustomerID, SalesOrderID,
    ROW_NUMBER() OVER(ORDER BY CustomerID) AS RowNumber
FROM Sales.SalesOrderHeader
ORDER BY SalesOrderID;
```

In this case, the row numbers are applied in order of the `CustomerID`, but the results are returned in order of `SalesOrderID`. The partial results are shown in Figure 1-4. In order to show that the row numbers are applied correctly, the figure shows the grid scrolled down to the first customer, `CustomerID` `11000`.

	CustomerID	SalesOrderID	RowNumber
135	11000	43793	1
136	11029	43794	87
137	27615	43795	25629
138	17956	43796	13624
139	16345	43797	11181

Figure 1-4. *Partial results of showing a query with a different ORDER BY than the OVER clause*

Just like the `ORDER BY` clause of a query, you can specify a descending order with the `DESCENDING` or `DESC` keyword within the `OVER` clause, as shown in Listing 1-4.

Listing 1-4. Using ROW_NUMBER with a Descending ORDER BY

```
--1-4.1 Row number with a descending ORDER BY
SELECT CustomerID, SalesOrderID,
    ROW_NUMBER() OVER(ORDER BY CustomerID DESC) AS RowNumber
FROM Sales.SalesOrderHeader;
```

Figure 1-5 shows partial results. Since it was easy for the database engine to return the results in descending order by `CustomerID`, you can easily see that row number 1 was applied to the largest `CustomerID`.

	CustomerID	SalesOrderID	RowNumber
1	30118	71803	1
2	30118	65221	2
3	30118	58928	3
4	30118	53480	4
5	30118	50675	5
6	30118	49499	6

Figure 1-5. *Partial results of ROW_NUMBER with a descending ORDER BY*

In the `SalesOrderHeader` table, the `CustomerID` is not unique. Notice in the last example that 30118 is the largest `CustomerID`. The row number with `SalesOrderID` 71803 is 1 and with 65221 is 2. There is no guarantee that the row numbers will be assigned exactly this way as long as the lowest RowNumbers are lined up with `CustomerID` 30118. To ensure that the row numbers line up as expected, use a unique column or combination of columns in the `ORDER BY` expression of the `OVER` clause. If you use more than one column, separate the columns with commas. You could even apply the row numbers in a random order. Listing 1-5 demonstrates this.

Listing 1-5. Using a Random Order with ROW_NUMBER

```
--1-5.1 Row number with a random ORDER BY
SELECT CustomerID, SalesOrderID,
    ROW_NUMBER() OVER(ORDER BY NEWID()) AS RowNumber
FROM Sales.SalesOrderHeader;
```

By using the `NEWID` function, the row numbers are applied in a random fashion. Figure 1-6 shows this. If you run the code, you will see different `CustomerID` values aligned with the row numbers. Each time the data is returned in order of row number, just because it is easy for the database engine to do so.

	CustomerID	SalesOrderID	RowNumber
1	26829	73862	1
2	19904	46515	2
3	29145	45189	3
4	30092	59067	4
5	25029	49245	5
6	13514	44011	6

Figure 1-6. *Partial results of ROW_NUMBER with a random ORDER BY*

As you may guess, applying the row numbers in a specific order involves sorting, which is an expensive operation. If you wish to generate row numbers but do not care about the order, you can use a subquery selecting a literal value in place of a column name. Listing 1-6 demonstrates how to do this.

Listing 1-6. Using ROW_NUMBER with No Order

```
--1-6.1 Use a constant for an ORDER BY
SELECT CustomerID, SalesOrderID,
    ROW_NUMBER() OVER(ORDER BY (SELECT 1)) AS RowNumber
FROM Sales.SalesOrderHeader;

--1-6.2 Apply an ORDER BY to the query
SELECT CustomerID, SalesOrderID,
    ROW_NUMBER() OVER(ORDER BY (SELECT 1)) AS RowNumber
FROM Sales.SalesOrderHeader
ORDER BY SalesOrderID;

--1-6.3 No ROW_NUMBER and no ORDER BY
SELECT CustomerID, SalesOrderID
FROM Sales.SalesOrderHeader;
```

Figure 1-7 shows the partial results. In Queries 1 and 2, a subquery selecting a constant replaces the ORDER BY column. The OVER clauses are identical, but the row numbers are applied differently, the easiest way possible. The difference between the two queries is that Query 2 has an ORDER BY clause. Since there is no specific order for the row numbers to be assigned, the easiest way is the order that the results would be returned even if the ROW_NUMBER function was not there. Query 3 shows how the rows are returned with no ROW_NUMBER and no ORDER BY. You may be wondering why the optimizer chose to return the results in Queries 1 and 3 in CustomerID order. There just happens to be a nonclustered index on CustomerID covering those queries. The optimizer chose the index that is ordered on CustomerID to solve the queries.

	CustomerID	SalesOrderID	RowNumber
1	11000	43793	1
2	11000	51522	2
3	11000	57418	3
4	11001	43767	4

	CustomerID	SalesOrderID	RowNumber
1	29825	43659	1
2	29672	43660	2
3	29734	43661	3
4	29994	43662	4

	CustomerID	SalesOrderID
1	11000	43793
2	11000	51522
3	11000	57418
4	11001	43767

Figure 1-7. *Partial results of letting the engine decide how row numbers are applied*

Another thing to learn from this example is that ROW_NUMBER is nondeterministic. It is not guaranteed to return the identical values under the same situations. By reviewing the documentation for each window function, you will see that each one is nondeterministic. You may argue that this is wrong because a different ORDER BY clause is used for the two queries, causing the two ROW_NUMBER functions to have different inputs. The article "Deterministic and Nondeterministic Functions" in SQL Server's documentation states:

> *You cannot influence the determinism of any built-in function. Each built-in function is deterministic or nondeterministic based on how the function is implemented by SQL Server. For example, specifying an ORDER BY clause in a query does not change the determinism of a function that is used in that query.*

If the ORDER BY clause consists of a unique set of columns, you can predict how the row numbers are assigned, but ROW_NUMBER is still nondeterministic. Listing 1-7 is an example.

Listing 1-7. Using Different ORDER BY Clauses

```
--1-7.1 OVER clause has just CustomerID
SELECT CustomerID, SalesOrderID,
    ROW_NUMBER() OVER(ORDER BY CustomerID) AS RowNumber
FROM Sales.SalesOrderHeader
ORDER BY CustomerID, SalesOrderID;

--1-7.2 Same query, just a new ORDER BY clause
SELECT CustomerID, SalesOrderID,
    ROW_NUMBER() OVER(ORDER BY CustomerID) AS RowNumber
FROM Sales.SalesOrderHeader
ORDER BY CustomerID, SalesOrderID DESC;
```

Figure 1-8 shows the partial results. Notice that SalesOrderID is assigned 1 in Query 1 and 3 in Query 2. The only difference between the two queries is the ORDER BY clause. Since CustomerID 11000 has three orders, numbers 1, 2, and 3 must be assigned to the three rows, but there is no guarantee how they will be assigned.

	CustomerID	SalesOrderID	RowNumber
1	11000	43793	1
2	11000	51522	2
3	11000	57418	3
4	11001	43767	4
	CustomerID	SalesOrderID	RowNumber
1	11000	57418	1
2	11000	51522	2
3	11000	43793	3
4	11001	72773	4

Figure 1-8. *Demonstrating nondeterminism*

There are a couple of things that you cannot do with window functions that may be related to determinism. You cannot use a window function expression in a computed column (a column in a table composed of an expression), and you cannot use a window function expression as a key for the clustered index of a view.

The ORDER BY expression in the OVER clause is quite versatile. You can use an expression instead of a column as was shown with NEWID in the earlier example. You can also list multiple columns or expressions. Listing 1-8 demonstrates using the CASE statement in the ORDER BY.

Listing 1-8. Using an Expression in the ORDER BY and Another Column

```
--1-8.1 Use an expression in the ORDER BY
SELECT CustomerID, SalesOrderID, OrderDate,
    ROW_NUMBER() OVER(ORDER BY CASE WHEN OrderDate > '2013/12/31'
        THEN 0 ELSE 1 END, SalesOrderID) AS RowNumber
FROM Sales.SalesOrderHeader;
```

Figure 1-9 shows the partial results. In this case, the row numbers are applied first to the orders from 2014 and then by SalesOrderID. The grid is scrolled down to the last three orders of 2014 so you can see that the next numbers applied are from the beginning of the data, 2011.

	CustomerID	SalesOrderID	OrderDate	RowNumber
11759	15251	75121	2014-06-30 00:00:00.000	11759
11760	15868	75122	2014-06-30 00:00:00.000	11760
11761	18759	75123	2014-06-30 00:00:00.000	11761
11762	29825	43659	2011-05-31 00:00:00.000	11762
11763	29672	43660	2011-05-31 00:00:00.000	11763
11764	29734	43661	2011-05-31 00:00:00.000	11764

Figure 1-9. *Partial results of using an expression and another column*

There are two additional components of the OVER clause: partitioning and framing. You will learn about framing, introduced in 2012, in Chapter 5. Partitioning divides the window into multiple, smaller windows, and you'll learn about that next.

Dividing Windows with Partitions

If there happens to be a window in the room you are sitting in, take a look at it now. Is it one large piece of glass, or is it divided into smaller panes? A window that is divided into panes is still a window. Each individual pane is also a window.

The same concept applies to window functions. The entire set of results is the window, but you can also divide the setup into smaller windows based on one or more columns. The OVER clause contains an optional component, PARTITION BY. When a PARTITION BY is not supplied, the partition is the entire large window.

The query using LAG to solve the stock market problem partitioned the data by the TickerSymbol column. By separating the data by TickerSymbol, the ClosePrice from one stock was not retrieved by rows of another stock. In the case of the ROW_NUMBER function demonstrated earlier in this chapter, you can force the numbers to start over at 1 for each customer, for example. Listing 1-9 demonstrates this feature.

Listing 1-9. Using PARTITION BY

```
--1-9.1 Use ROW_NUMBER with PARTITION BY
SELECT CustomerID, SalesOrderID,
    ROW_NUMBER() OVER(PARTITION BY CustomerID ORDER BY SalesOrderID)
    AS RowNumber
FROM Sales.SalesOrderHeader;
```

Figure 1-10 shows partial results. Notice that the row numbers start over at 1 for each customer.

	CustomerID	SalesOrderID	RowNumber
1	11000	43793	1
2	11000	51522	2
3	11000	57418	3
4	11001	43767	1
5	11001	51493	2
6	11001	72773	3
7	11002	43736	1

Figure 1-10. *Partial results of using the PARTITION BY option with ROW_NUMBER*

15

The PARTITION BY expression of the OVER clause is supported by all window functions. It is also always optional. If the PARTITION BY is left out, all rows are included in the window. When the PARTITION BY is used, each window will consist only of the rows matching the PARTITION BY column or columns.

Uncovering Special Case Windows

So far, the examples have been straightforward, but there are some situations that are counterintuitive if you don't know what is going on. The examples in this section use the ROW_NUMBER function, but the concepts apply to any window function.

First, take a look at what happens when the DISTINCT keyword is used with ROW_ NUMBER. The window function operates before DISTINCT, which can lead to results you may not expect. Listing 1-10 demonstrates using DISTINCT with ROW_NUMBER to get a list of the unique OrderDates along with a row number.

Listing 1-10. Using DISTINCT with ROW_NUMBER

```
--1-10.1 Using DISTINCT
SELECT DISTINCT OrderDate,
    ROW_NUMBER() OVER(ORDER BY OrderDate) AS RowNumber
FROM Sales.SalesOrderHeader
ORDER BY RowNumber;

--1-10.2 Separate logic with CTE
WITH OrderDates AS (
    SELECT DISTINCT OrderDate
    FROM Sales.SalesOrderHeader)
SELECT OrderDate,
    ROW_NUMBER() OVER(ORDER BY OrderDate) AS RowNumber
FROM OrderDates
ORDER BY RowNumber;
```

Figure 1-11 shows the partial results. Query 1 returns 31,465 rows, one row for each order in the table even though many orders have the same date. This is definitely not the intended answer. The row numbers are generated before DISTINCT is applied. Because the row numbers are unique, every row in the results ends up being unique, and DISTINCT cannot eliminate any rows. Query 2 demonstrates the solution: get a distinct list of the order dates first in a CTE, and then apply the row numbers in the outer query. Query 2 returns 1124 rows, the number of unique order dates. You could also use a temp table, a table variable, a view, or a derived table to create the distinct list first.

	OrderDate	RowNumber
1	2011-05-31 00:00:00.000	1
2	2011-05-31 00:00:00.000	2
3	2011-05-31 00:00:00.000	3
4	2011-05-31 00:00:00.000	4
5	2011-05-31 00:00:00.000	5
6	2011-05-31 00:00:00.000	6
7	2011-05-31 00:00:00.000	7
8	2011-05-31 00:00:00.000	8

	OrderDate	RowNumber
1	2011-05-31 00:00:00.000	1
2	2011-06-01 00:00:00.000	2
3	2011-06-02 00:00:00.000	3
4	2011-06-03 00:00:00.000	4
5	2011-06-04 00:00:00.000	5
6	2011-06-05 00:00:00.000	6
7	2011-06-06 00:00:00.000	7
8	2011-06-07 00:00:00.000	8

Figure 1-11. *Partial results of using DISTINCT with ROW_NUMBER*

You will also find interesting behavior when you use TOP. Once again, the row numbers are generated before TOP is applied. I first discovered this when I was inserting random rows into a table for some unit tests. The idea was to reinsert a sample of rows back into the same table with new ID numbers. To generate the new IDs, I wanted to add row numbers to the maximum existing ID. Since I wanted to insert a specific number of rows, I used TOP. Instead of the row numbers starting with one as I expected, they started with a random value. Listing 1-11 shows how using TOP can affect window functions.

Listing 1-11. Using TOP with ROW_NUMBER

```
--1-11.1 Using TOP with ROW_NUMBER
SELECT TOP(6) CustomerID, SalesOrderID,
    ROW_NUMBER() OVER(ORDER BY SalesOrderID) AS RowNumber
FROM Sales.SalesOrderHeader
ORDER BY NEWID();

--1-11.2 Separate the logic with a CTE
WITH Orders AS (
    SELECT TOP(6) CustomerID, SalesOrderID
    FROM Sales.SalesOrderHeader
    ORDER BY NEWID())
SELECT CustomerID, SalesOrderID,
    ROW_NUMBER() OVER(ORDER BY SalesOrderID) AS RowNumber
FROM Orders;
```

Figure 1-12 shows the results. If you run this example, you will see different random results. The purpose of the example is to generate six random rows with a row number starting with 1. Query 1 returns row numbers, but the row numbers do not start with one nor are they in any kind of order. By using a CTE to separate the logic, TOP can operate first. Query 2 returns a random set of rows, but the row numbers start with one as expected.

	CustomerID	SalesOrderID	RowNumber
1	15734	71756	28098
2	17977	50165	6507
3	15575	72626	28968
4	30086	63172	19514
5	23777	57297	13639
6	12314	49330	5672

	CustomerID	SalesOrderID	RowNumber
1	27920	43996	1
2	25226	51025	2
3	28084	65819	3
4	13356	68499	4
5	17453	71538	5
6	12330	73865	6

Figure 1-12. *The results of using TOP with ROW_NUMBER*

The final interesting situation involves adding window functions to aggregate queries. This functionality is covered in Chapter 3 in the "Adding Window Aggregates to Aggregate Queries" section.

Summary

Window functions, added with SQL Server 2005 and 2012, provide new, easy ways to solve challenging queries. Window functions are part of the ANSI standards for SQL. The standards committee has defined even more functionality, so it's possible that Microsoft may include additional functions in the future. Window functions must include an OVER clause, which defines the window for each row to operate on. Depending on the window function used, the OVER clause may contain ORDER BY and frame expressions. The PARTITION BY expression is supported in all window functions and will be used depending on the desired outcome. In many cases, using a window function provides better performance over older methods, but they almost always make the query easier to write.

Now that you understand the basics of window functions, it is time to investigate ranking functions. In Chapter 2, you will learn how to use the four ranking functions introduced with SQL Server 2005 to solve challenging T-SQL queries.

CHAPTER 2

Discovering Ranking Functions

The four ranking functions were introduced to T-SQL by Microsoft in 2005. Three of the functions, ROW_NUMBER, RANK, and DENSE_RANK, assign a sequential number to each row in a query's results. The fourth ranking function, NTILE, divides the rows by assigning a bucket number to each row in the results. The group of low-ranking rows gets an NTILE value of 1 while the highest-ranking group of rows is assigned the top number.

While adding a number to a row is not generally the answer in itself, this functionality is often the basis for many solutions. This chapter shows how to use the four ranking functions and how to apply them to some real-world problems in this chapter and later chapters of this book.

Using ROW_NUMBER

Based on my asking audiences at SQL Server events, ROW_NUMBER is the most well-known and commonly used window function. Many SQL Server professionals admit to using ROW_NUMBER even if they do not realize it is one of the window functions. You saw ROW_NUMBER in action in Chapter 1 when you learned about the OVER clause. Now you will take an even deeper look at ROW_NUMBER.

The ROW_NUMBER function returns a unique integer starting with one for each row in the window. An ORDER BY expression inside the OVER clause is required, and it determines the order in which the numbers are applied. All the window functions support an optional PARTITION BY expression that divides the window into smaller windows. The row number for each partition begins with 1 and increments by 1.

21

© Kathi Kellenberger, Clayton Groom, and Ed Pollack 2019
K. Kellenberger et al., *Expert T-SQL Window Functions in SQL Server 2019*,
https://doi.org/10.1007/978-1-4842-5197-3_2

Here is the basic syntax for ROW_NUMBER, which may appear in the SELECT list and
ORDER BY clause of a query:

```
ROW_NUMBER() OVER([PARTITION BY <col1>[,<col2>,...<n>]]
ORDER BY <col3> [,<col4>,...<n>])
```

Listing 2-1 demonstrates ROW_NUMBER with and without a PARTITION BY expression.
So that the row numbers line up by CustomerID for comparison, the ORDER BY
expressions of the OVER clauses are different.

Listing 2-1. Using ROW_NUMBER With and Without a PARTITION BY

```
--2-1.1 Using ROW_NUMBER with and without a PARTITION BY
SELECT CustomerID, CAST(OrderDate AS DATE)
    AS OrderDate, SalesOrderID,
    ROW_NUMBER() OVER(PARTITION BY CustomerID ORDER BY SalesOrderID)
        AS WithPart,
    ROW_NUMBER() OVER(ORDER BY CustomerID) AS WithoutPart
FROM Sales.SalesOrderHeader;
```

Figure 2-1 shows the partial results. The row number columns, WithPart and
WithoutPart, are the same values for the first three rows, CustomerID 11000. After that,
the WithPart rows start over for each new CustomerID because of the PARTITION BY
expression.

	CustomerID	OrderDate	SalesOrderID	WithPart	WithoutPart
1	11000	2011-06-21	43793	1	1
2	11000	2013-06-20	51522	2	2
3	11000	2013-10-03	57418	3	3
4	11001	2011-06-17	43767	1	4
5	11001	2013-06-18	51493	2	5
6	11001	2014-05-12	72773	3	6
7	11002	2011-06-09	43736	1	7
8	11002	2013-06-02	51238	2	8

Figure 2-1. *Partial results of ROW_NUMBER with and without partitioning*

There is another interesting thing to consider with this query. The ORDER BY expression in the second OVER clause, CustomerID, is not unique in this data. Both the row numbers for SalesOrderID 43793 return 1. It's possible for the WithoutPart value to be 2 or 3 for that row since there are three orders for CustomerID 11000 and the ORDER BY expression is based just on that column. The row numbers are applied correctly since they are in order of CustomerID, but since CustomerID is not unique, the order in which the numbers are applied within CustomerID is not guaranteed. The WithoutPart value for SalesOrderID 43793 could be 1, 2, or 3. In Chapter 1, I mentioned briefly that all window functions are nondeterministic, and Listing 2-2 demonstrates how different row numbers are possible with the same OVER clause.

Listing 2-2. Different Row Numbers with the Same OVER Clause

```
--2-2.1 Query ORDER BY ascending
SELECT CustomerID,
    CAST(OrderDate AS DATE) AS OrderDate,
    SalesOrderID,
    ROW_NUMBER() OVER(ORDER BY CustomerID) AS RowNumber
FROM Sales.SalesOrderHeader
ORDER BY CustomerID, SalesOrderID;

--2-2.2 Query ORDER BY descending
SELECT CustomerID,
    CAST(OrderDate AS DATE) AS OrderDate,
    SalesOrderID,
    ROW_NUMBER() OVER(ORDER BY CustomerID) AS RowNumber
FROM Sales.SalesOrderHeader
ORDER BY CustomerID, SalesOrderID DESC;
```

Figure 2-2 shows the partial results. The OVER clauses are identical, but the queries are sorted differently. The row number for SalesOrderID 43793 in Query 1 is 1, but the row number is 3 in Query 2.

	CustomerID	OrderDate	SalesOrderID	RowNumber
1	11000	2011-06-21	43793	1
2	11000	2013-06-20	51522	2
3	11000	2013-10-03	57418	3
4	11001	2011-06-17	43767	4
	CustomerID	OrderDate	SalesOrderID	RowNumber
1	11000	2013-10-03	57418	1
2	11000	2013-06-20	51522	2
3	11000	2011-06-21	43793	3
4	11001	2014-05-12	72773	4

Figure 2-2. *Different results with nonunique ORDER BY in the OVER clause*

This proves that ROW_NUMBER is nondeterministic; in other words, you can get different values from the function under the same circumstances. The ORDER BY clause of the query doesn't affect determinism, so this is a valid test.

To ensure repeatable results when using ROW_NUMBER, actually with any of the window functions, make sure that the ORDER BY columns in the OVER clause are unique. Listing 2-3 is an example using multiple ORDER BY columns so that the expression is unique.

Listing 2-3. Using Multiple Columns in the ORDER BY Expression to Ensure Uniqueness

```
--2-3.1 Using ROW_NUMBER a unique ORDER BY
SELECT CustomerID,
       CAST(OrderDate AS DATE) AS OrderDate,
       SalesOrderID,
    ROW_NUMBER() OVER(ORDER BY CustomerID, SalesOrderID) AS RowNum
FROM Sales.SalesOrderHeader
ORDER BY CustomerID, SalesOrderID;
```

```
--2-3.2 Change to descending
SELECT CustomerID,
       CAST(OrderDate AS Date) AS OrderDate,
       SalesOrderID,
    ROW_NUMBER() OVER(ORDER BY CustomerID, SalesOrderID) AS RowNum
FROM Sales.SalesOrderHeader
ORDER BY CustomerID, SalesOrderID DESC;
```

Figure 2-3 shows the partial results. In this case, SaleOrderID 43793 has a
row number of 1 regardless of the query's ORDER BY clause. ROW_NUMBER is still a
nondeterministic function, but the assignments are consistent because of the unique
ORDER BY columns.

	CustomerID	OrderDate	SalesOrderID	RowNum
1	11000	2011-06-21	43793	1
2	11000	2013-06-20	51522	2
3	11000	2013-10-03	57418	3
4	11001	2011-06-17	43767	4
	CustomerID	OrderDate	SalesOrderID	RowNum
1	11000	2013-10-03	57418	3
2	11000	2013-06-20	51522	2
3	11000	2011-06-21	43793	1
4	11001	2014-05-12	72773	6

Figure 2-3. *Using a unique ORDER BY expression in the OVER clause*

It is also possible to have multiple columns, expressions, and subqueries in the
PARTITION BY expression of the OVER clause. In fact, as you will see in the "Solving
Queries with Ranking Functions" section at the end of this chapter, multiple columns in
the PARTITION BY is the key to solving some real-world examples.

With ROW_NUMBER, the database engine sorts the rows in each partition and assigns
unique numbers based on the position of each row. You have seen situations where the
ORDER BY expression of OVER is not unique, so the row numbers are not guaranteed to
line up exactly the same each time when there are ties in the values. Now you will learn
about two functions that handle ties differently: RANK and DENSE_RANK.

Understanding RANK and DENSE_RANK

The functions RANK and DENSE_RANK look very similar to ROW_NUMBER. In fact, in many queries they will return exactly the same values as ROW_NUMBER. The RANK and DENSE_RANK functions are quite different, however, since instead of just assigning sequential numbers, they rank the rows based on the ORDER BY expression.

The difference shows up when the ORDER BY column of the OVER clause is not unique. For example, many customers could place orders on the same date, but each order has a unique SalesOrderID. If you used the OrderDate column instead of the SalesOrderID, you will see ties in the results. The ranking of the rows with ties will be the same.

There is also a difference between RANK and DENSE_RANK. The RANK function returns the rank of the current row compared to the position of all the rows of the partition. The DENSE_RANK function returns the rank based on the unique value of the ORDER BY expression of the current row in the partition. RANK says how many rows before the current one, and DENSE_RANK says how many *unique values* come before the current value. Another way to think about this is ROW_NUMBER is positional, DENSE_RANK is logical, and RANK is halfway between the two. ROW_NUMBER is based on the position of the row when it is lined up, and DENSE_RANK is based on how the unique value lines up.

The syntax of these two functions looks a lot like the syntax of ROW_NUMBER:

```
RANK() OVER([PARTITION BY <col1>[,<col2>,...<n>]]
ORDER BY <col3> [,<col4>,...<n>])
```

```
DENSE_RANK() OVER([PARTITION BY <col1>[,<col2>,...<n>]]
ORDER BY <col3> [,<col4>,...<n>])
```

Listing 2-4 compares ROW_NUMBER to RANK and DENSE_RANK. The query is filtered to show to customers who have placed multiple orders on the same date.

Listing 2-4. Using RANK and DENSE_RANK

```
--2-4.1 Using RANK and DENSE_RANK
SELECT CustomerID, CAST(OrderDate AS DATE) AS OrderDate,
    ROW_NUMBER() OVER(ORDER BY OrderDate) AS RowNumber,
    RANK() OVER(ORDER BY OrderDate) AS [Rank],
    DENSE_RANK() OVER(ORDER BY OrderDate) AS DenseRank
FROM Sales.SalesOrderHeader
WHERE CustomerID IN (11330, 29676);
```

Figure 2-4 shows the partial results. The ORDER BY column in each OVER clause is OrderDate which is not unique. The row numbers are unique and sequential, just as expected. Notice that the Rank values of the third and fourth rows are both 3. Both of those rows have the OrderDate of 2013-07-31, a tie. This is the third ranked OrderDate in the set of rows. On row 5, the Rank "catches up" with the RowNumber value, 5. The date 2013-08-09 in the fifth row is the fifth ranked OrderDate in the set.

	CustomerID	OrderDate	RowNumber	Rank	DenseRank
1	11330	2013-07-15	1	1	1
2	11330	2013-07-26	2	2	2
3	29676	2013-07-31	3	3	3
4	29676	2013-07-31	4	3	3
5	11330	2013-08-09	5	5	4
6	11330	2013-10-11	6	6	5
7	11330	2013-10-16	7	7	6
8	11330	2013-10-24	8	8	7
9	11330	2013-10-24	9	8	7

Figure 2-4. Partial results comparing ROW_NUMBER, RANK, and DENSE_RANK

The DenseRank values for rows 3 and 4 are also both 3. Notice that the DenseRank for row 5 is 4, however. The date 2013-08-09 is the fourth *distinct* OrderDate in the set.

The ROW_NUMBER, RANK, and DENSE_RANK functions assign a number to each row. Now you will learn about a different type of ranking function, NTILE.

Dividing Data with NTILE

The NTILE function is a ranking function, but with a twist. The numbers applied are used to divide the results into equal buckets. You must specify how many buckets are needed and, just like the other ranking functions, an ORDER BY expression is required in the OVER clause. Here is the syntax for NTILE:

```
NTILE(<buckets>) OVER([PARTITION BY <col1>[,<col2>,...<n>]]
ORDER BY <col3> [,<col4>,...<n>])
```

Within the parentheses after the word NTILE, supply the number of buckets you want to see in the results. The PARTITION BY expression is optional, and the ORDER BY is required. Listing 2-5 shows an example that divides the months into four buckets depending on the sales of 2013.

Listing 2-5. Using NTILE

```
--2.5.1 Using NTILE
WITH Orders AS (
    SELECT MONTH(OrderDate) AS OrderMonth,
        FORMAT(SUM(TotalDue),'C') AS Sales
    FROM Sales.SalesOrderHeader
    WHERE OrderDate >= '2013/01/01' and OrderDate < '2014/01/01'
        GROUP BY MONTH(OrderDate))
SELECT OrderMonth, Sales, NTILE(4) OVER(ORDER BY Sales) AS Bucket
FROM Orders;
```

Figure 2-5 shows the results. The query aggregates the sales from 2013 into months inside a CTE called Orders. In the outer query, the NTILE function is applied. The bucket that each month falls into depends on the sales for that month. Bucket #1 contains the three months with the lowest sales. Bucket #4 contains the three months with the highest sales.

	OrderMonth	Sales	Bucket
1	1	$2,340,061.55	1
2	2	$2,600,218.87	1
3	4	$2,840,711.17	1
4	5	$3,658,084.95	2
5	11	$3,694,668.00	2
6	8	$3,733,973.00	2
7	3	$3,831,605.94	3
8	12	$4,560,577.10	3
9	9	$5,083,505.34	3
10	10	$5,374,375.94	4
11	7	$5,521,840.84	4
12	6	$5,726,265.26	4

Figure 2-5. *Using NTILE*

In this example, using four buckets, the data divided up evenly into the buckets. Sometimes the rows are not evenly divided by the bucket number. When there is one extra row after dividing, bucket #1 will get an extra row. When there are two extra rows after dividing, buckets #1 and #2 will get an extra row and so on. Listing 2-6 demonstrates this.

Listing 2-6. Using NTILE with Uneven Buckets

```
--2.6.1 Using NTILE with uneven buckets
WITH Orders AS (
    SELECT MONTH(OrderDate) AS OrderMonth, FORMAT(SUM(TotalDue),'C')
        AS Sales
    FROM Sales.SalesOrderHeader
    WHERE OrderDate >= '2013/01/01' and OrderDate < '2014/01/01'
    GROUP BY MONTH(OrderDate))
SELECT OrderMonth, Sales, NTILE(5) OVER(ORDER BY Sales) AS Bucket
FROM Orders;
```

	OrderMonth	Sales	Bucket
1	1	$2,340,061.55	1
2	2	$2,600,218.87	1
3	4	$2,840,711.17	1
4	5	$3,658,084.95	2
5	11	$3,694,668.00	2
6	8	$3,733,973.00	2
7	3	$3,831,605.94	3
8	12	$4,560,577.10	3
9	9	$5,083,505.34	4
10	10	$5,374,375.94	4
11	7	$5,521,840.84	5
12	6	$5,726,265.26	5

Figure 2-6. *The results of NTILE with uneven buckets*

This query returns five buckets. Twelve divided by five is two with a remainder of two. If you take a look at the results shown in Figure 2-6, you will see that buckets #1 and #2 each have three rows. The other buckets each have two rows.

You have seen many examples explaining how to use the ranking functions in this chapter, but you have not seen any practical examples. The next section will demonstrate some real-world problems that can be solved with these functions.

Solving Queries with Ranking Functions

Since 2005 when these functions were first introduced, I have found more and more reasons to use the ranking functions when writing queries. I believe they have helped me learn to think in a set-based manner, and using window functions just became intuitive over time. When I am faced with a challenging query, I often just add a row number to see if I can find any patterns and go from there.

Deduplicating Data

There is always more than one way to solve a problem, and deduplicating data is a good example. The traditional approach involves storing the distinct rows in a temp table. Then you can truncate the original table and insert the rows back in from the temp table. There could be a situation in which you cannot empty the original table and must selectively delete the extra rows. You can solve this problem using a row number. Listing 2-7 creates a table with duplicate rows.

Listing 2-7. Creating a Table with Duplicate Rows

```
--2-7.1 Create a table that will hold duplicate rows
CREATE TABLE #dupes(Col1 INT, Col2 CHAR(1));

--2-7.2 Insert some rows
INSERT INTO #dupes(Col1, Col2)
VALUES (1,'a'),(1,'a'),(2,'b'),
    (3,'c'),(4,'d'),(4,'d'),(5,'e');

--2-7.3
SELECT Col1, Col2
FROM #dupes;
```

Figure 2-7 shows the results. You can see that several rows are duplicates. In real life, the table will probably have more columns, but two columns are enough to demonstrate this technique.

	Col1	Col2
1	1	a
2	1	a
3	2	b
4	3	c
5	4	d
6	4	d
7	5	e

Figure 2-7. *The table with duplicate rows*

Listing 2-8 contains a script to remove the duplicates. To better understand how this works, it is broken down into two steps. Be sure to run this code in the same query window as Listing 2-7 so that the temp table is in place.

Listing 2-8. Removing the Duplicate Rows

```
--2-8.1 Add ROW_NUMBER and Partition by all of the columns
SELECT Col1, Col2,
    ROW_NUMBER() OVER(PARTITION BY Col1, Col2 ORDER BY Col1) AS RowNumber
FROM #dupes;

--2-8.2 Delete the rows with RowNumber > 1
WITH Dupes AS (
    SELECT Col1, Col2,
        ROW_NUMBER() OVER(PARTITION BY Col1, Col2 ORDER BY Col1)
            AS RowNumber
    FROM #dupes)
DELETE Dupes WHERE RowNumber > 1;

--2-8.3 The results
SELECT Col1, Col2
FROM #dupes;
```

Figure 2-8 shows the results of running this script. A ROW_NUMBER function is added to Query 1. To get the row numbers to start over for each unique row, partition by all of the columns in the table. This table has only two columns, but if it had more, they would all be listed in the PARTITION BY expression. Since the row numbers start over for each unique row, it is easy to see the rows to delete: they all have row numbers greater than 1. Statement 2 deletes those rows. Because you cannot add the ROW_NUMBER function to the WHERE clause, the logic is separated by adding the row number in a CTE. The duplicates are deleted directly from the CTE. Finally, Query 3 demonstrates that the duplicates are gone.

	Col1	Col2	RowNumber
1	1	a	1
2	1	a	2
3	2	b	1
4	3	c	1
5	4	d	1
6	4	d	2
7	5	e	1

	Col1	Col2
1	1	a
2	2	b
3	3	c
4	4	d
5	5	e

Figure 2-8. Removing duplicate rows

Finding the First N Rows of Every Group

I first thought about this problem during a technical interview. The potential customer wanted to know how I would find the first four orders of every month within a particular year. One method of solving it involves using CROSS APPLY and TOP. The solution that is easiest to write uses ROW_NUMBER. Listing 2-9 shows both methods.

Listing 2-9. Finding the First Four Orders of Each Month

```
--2-9.1 Using CROSS APPLY to find the first four orders
WITH Months AS (
    SELECT MONTH(OrderDate) AS OrderMonth
    FROM Sales.SalesOrderHeader
    WHERE OrderDate >= '2013-01-01' AND OrderDate < '2014-01-01'
    GROUP BY MONTH(OrderDate))
SELECT OrderMonth, CAST(CA.OrderDate AS DATE) AS OrderDate,
    CA.SalesOrderID, CA.TotalDue
FROM Months
```

```
CROSS APPLY (
    SELECT TOP(4) SalesOrderID, OrderDate, TotalDue
    FROM Sales.SalesOrderHeader AS IQ
    WHERE OrderDate >= '2013-01-01' AND OrderDate < '2014-01-01'
        AND MONTH(IQ.OrderDate) =MONTHS.OrderMonth
    ORDER BY SalesOrderID) AS CA
ORDER BY OrderMonth, SalesOrderID;

--2-9.2 Use ROW_NUMBER to find the first four orders
WITH Orders AS (
    SELECT  MONTH(OrderDate) AS OrderMonth, OrderDate,
        SalesOrderID, TotalDue,
        ROW_NUMBER() OVER(PARTITION BY MONTH(OrderDate)
            ORDER BY SalesOrderID) AS RowNumber
    FROM Sales.SalesOrderHeader
    WHERE OrderDate >= '2013-01-01' AND OrderDate < '2014-01-01')
SELECT OrderMonth, CAST(OrderDate AS DATE) AS OrderDate,
    SalesOrderID, TotalDue
FROM Orders
WHERE RowNumber <= 4
ORDER BY OrderMonth, SalesOrderID;
```

Figure 2-9 shows the partial results, the rows for January and February. A total of 48 rows were returned for each query. Query 1 is complex. In my opinion, it is not easy to figure out. The CTE creates a list of months for sales year 2013. The outer query joins the Months CTE to an inner query using CROSS APPLY. In order to pull back the first four rows for each row of the outer query, TOP is used. CROSS APPLY must be used in this case because using a derived table will just pull back a total of four rows, not four rows for each month.

	OrderMonth	OrderDate	SalesOrderID	TotalDue
1	1	2013-01-01	49181	2410.6266
2	1	2013-01-01	49182	2699.9018
3	1	2013-01-01	49183	2699.9018
4	1	2013-01-01	49184	2264.2536
5	2	2013-02-01	49581	2699.9018
6	2	2013-02-01	49582	2410.6266
7	2	2013-02-01	49583	2410.6266
8	2	2013-02-01	49584	2699.9018

	OrderMonth	OrderDate	SalesOrderID	TotalDue
1	1	2013-01-01	49181	2410.6266
2	1	2013-01-01	49182	2699.9018
3	1	2013-01-01	49183	2699.9018
4	1	2013-01-01	49184	2264.2536
5	2	2013-02-01	49581	2699.9018
6	2	2013-02-01	49582	2410.6266
7	2	2013-02-01	49583	2410.6266
8	2	2013-02-01	49584	2699.9018

Figure 2-9. Partial results of returning the first four sales of each month

Query 2 uses ROW_NUMBER to accomplish the same thing. The CTE contains all of the expressions needed in the results plus a row number. The row number is partitioned by month, so that the numbers start over for each month. The outer query simply retrieves the data from the CTE and filters on the row number.

For another twist on this problem, what about finding the four orders from each month with the highest price? Listing 2-10 shows how to write this query.

Listing 2-10. Finding the Four Most Expensive Orders Each Month

```
--2-10.1 Use ROW_NUMBER to find the first four orders
WITH Orders AS (
    SELECT  MONTH(OrderDate) AS OrderMonth, OrderDate,
        SalesOrderID, TotalDue,
```

```
        ROW_NUMBER() OVER(PARTITION BY MONTH(OrderDate)
            ORDER BY TotalDue DESC) AS RowNumber
    FROM Sales.SalesOrderHeader
    WHERE OrderDate >= '2013-01-01' AND OrderDate < '2014-01-01')
SELECT OrderMonth, CAST(OrderDate AS DATE) AS OrderDate,
    SalesOrderID,
    TotalDue
FROM Orders
WHERE RowNumber <= 4
ORDER BY OrderMonth, TotalDue DESC;
```

Figure 2-10 shows the partial results. In this case, four orders from each month are returned and these are the highest sales for each month.

	OrderMonth	OrderDate	SalesOrderID	TotalDue
1	1	2013-01-28	49509	101069.7604
2	1	2013-01-28	49485	97224.9592
3	1	2013-01-28	49479	90736.4249
4	1	2013-01-28	49498	64243.0161
5	2	2013-02-28	49884	110266.9588
6	2	2013-02-28	49888	108780.5231
7	2	2013-02-28	49837	100902.437
8	2	2013-02-28	49828	99507.5528

Figure 2-10. *Partial results of the four most expensive orders each month*

You could also use this technique to find rows at a specific position or a range of rows such as for paging. For example, you may need to display ten rows at a time on a web page. It's easy to just supply a variable for the first and last rows you want to display in the WHERE clause after adding a row number to the query in a CTE. There is another method that might work better, the OFFSET/FETCH technique that was first available with SQL Server 2012. This is an option for the ORDER BY clause, and more information can be found here: https://docs.microsoft.com/en-us/sql/t-sql/queries/select-order-by-clause-transact-sql?view=sql-server-2017

Creating a Tally Table

There are many problems where a tally table, or table of numbers, can come in handy, and there are also several methods to create such a table. Listing 2-11 shows an example script that uses ROW_NUMBER.

Listing 2-11. Creating a Numbers Table

```
--2-11.1 Create the table
CREATE TABLE #Numbers(Number INT);

--2-11.2 Populate the tally table
INSERT INTO #Numbers(Number)
SELECT TOP(1000000) ROW_NUMBER() OVER(ORDER BY a.object_id)
FROM sys.objects a
CROSS JOIN sys.objects b
CROSS JOIN sys.objects c;
```

By using CROSS JOIN, you can generate a large number of rows, in this case limited to one million with TOP. Then by adding ROW_NUMBER, the numbers 1 to 1,000,000 will be added to the table.

Now that you have a tally table, you might wonder what you will do with it. A tally table often comes in handy when you need to find missing dates or ID numbers in a table. Listing 2-12 is an example. Be sure to run in the query window where the tally table was created.

Listing 2-12. Using the Tally Table to Find Dates with No Orders

```
--2-12.1 Find the earliest date and the number of days
DECLARE @Min DATE, @DayCount INT;
SELECT @Min = MIN(OrderDate),
       @DayCount = DATEDIFF(DAY,MIN(OrderDate),MAX(OrderDate))
FROM Sales.SalesOrderHeader;

--2-12.2 Change numbers to dates and then find missing
WITH Dates AS (
       SELECT TOP(@DayCount) DATEADD(DAY,Number,@Min) AS OrderDate
       FROM #Numbers AS N
       ORDER BY Number
)
```

```
SELECT Dates.OrderDate
FROM Dates
LEFT JOIN Sales.SalesOrderHeader AS SOH
        ON Dates.OrderDate = SOH.OrderDate
WHERE SOH.SalesOrderID IS NULL;
```

This example first finds the minimum date in the table and difference between the minimum and maximum dates. It then uses a CTE to convert the numbers to dates starting with the day after the earliest date. In the outer query, it compares the Dates CTE to the table, joining on OrderDate and finding the rows that are NULL. Figure 2-11 shows the results. There are three dates that do not have any orders.

	OrderDate
1	2011-08-11
2	2011-09-23
3	2011-07-16

Figure 2-11. *The dates with no orders*

Solving the Bonus Problem

This example is one that I have used over the years to explain how to use the NTILE function. Imagine that you are a manager with a team of salespeople. You have bonus money to give out and want to divide the money based on how much each person has sold. The best performing group of salespeople will each get $4000, and the least performing group will get $1000. Listing 2-13 shows how to solve this problem using NTILE.

Listing 2-13. Solving the Bonus Problem

```
--2-13.1 Using NTILE to assign bonuses
WITH Sales AS (
    SELECT SP.FirstName, SP.LastName,
        SUM(SOH.TotalDue) AS TotalSales
    FROM [Sales].[vSalesPerson] SP
```

```
JOIN Sales.SalesOrderHeader SOH
        ON SP.BusinessEntityID = SOH.SalesPersonID
    WHERE SOH.OrderDate >= '2011-01-01' AND SOH.OrderDate < '2012-01-01'
    GROUP BY FirstName, LastName)
SELECT FirstName, LastName, TotalSales,
    NTILE(4) OVER(ORDER BY TotalSales) * 1000 AS Bonus
FROM Sales;
```

Figure 2-12 shows the results. This query filters for just one year, 2011. The data is aggregated, and the sum of TotalSales is calculated for each person inside a CTE called Sales. In the outer query, the NTILE function divides the rows into four buckets. The number of buckets is designated by the argument provided to NTILE. By multiplying the bucket number by 1000, the bonus is returned. The salespeople with the lowest sales get the smaller bonus.

	FirstName	LastName	TotalSales	Bonus
1	Stephen	Jiang	32567.9155	1000
2	Garrett	Vargas	563326.5478	1000
3	David	Campbell	675663.694	1000
4	Pamela	Ansman-Wolfe	730273.4889	2000
5	Michael	Blythe	986298.0902	2000
6	Shu	Ito	1089874.3906	2000
7	Linda	Mitchell	1294819.7439	3000
8	José	Saraiva	1323328.6346	3000
9	Jillian	Carson	1477158.2811	4000
10	Tsvi	Reiter	1713640.8372	4000

Figure 2-12. *The results of the bonus problem*

You may have noticed that there are three people in the first two groups and just two people in the last two groups. This is because ten cannot be evenly divided by four. One row of the remainder is added to each of the first two groups. In this case, two people get the top bonus, but what if you wanted to move the remainder rows to the top performing groups? You can sort the rows in descending order to move the extra rows, but then there is the problem of how to calculate the bonus. By dusting off the algebraic formula for a line, y = mx + b, it's possible to get the right results. The slope of the line (m) is -1000 and the intersect (b) is 5000. Listing 2-14 shows that this can be done.

Listing 2-14. Use Algebra to Give Three People the Best Bonus

```
--2-14.1 Assign bonuses in opposite order
WITH Sales AS (
    SELECT SP.FirstName, SP.LastName,
        SUM(SOH.TotalDue) AS TotalSales
    FROM [Sales].[vSalesPerson] SP
    JOIN Sales.SalesOrderHeader SOH
            ON SP.BusinessEntityID = SOH.SalesPersonID
    WHERE SOH.OrderDate >= '2011-01-01' AND SOH.OrderDate < '2012-01-01'
    GROUP BY FirstName, LastName)
SELECT FirstName, LastName, TotalSales,
    -1000 * NTILE(4) OVER(ORDER BY TotalSales DESC) + 5000 AS Bonus
FROM Sales;
```

Figure 2-13 shows the results. By sorting in the opposite direction and then multiplying the result of NTILE by -1000 and adding 5000, three people get the best bonus.

	FirstName	LastName	TotalSales	Bonus
1	Ken	Sánchez	4268747.9012	4000
2	Tsvi	Reiter	1713640.8372	4000
3	Jillian	Carson	1477158.2811	4000
4	José	Saraiva	1323328.6346	3000
5	Linda	Mitchell	1294819.7439	3000
6	Shu	Ito	1089874.3906	3000
7	Michael	Blythe	986298.0902	2000
8	Pamela	Ansman-Wolfe	730273.4889	2000
9	David	Campbell	675663.694	2000
10	Garrett	Vargas	563326.5478	1000
11	Stephen	Jiang	32567.9155	1000

Figure 2-13. *The results when giving three people the best bonus*

I've also heard about shops using NTILE to divide up results of contests or groups of donors. It's not used often, but just keep it in mind if there is a reason that it will be useful.

Summary

The ranking functions, ROW_NUMBER, RANK, DENSE_RANK, and NTILE, are the most basic of all the window functions. The ranking functions add a number to each row of the results. The ORDER BY expression of the OVER clause is required, and, depending on the situation, you may also want to add PARTITION BY. These functions are usually not the solution in themselves but often form the basis of a more complex solution.

When faced with a tricky query, you may want to add a row number to look for patterns or relationships between the rows. Then use those patterns and relationships to figure out the solution. You'll see the ranking functions used to solve more query problems in Chapters 9 and 10.

Chapter 3 covers window aggregates, which allow you to add functions like SUM or AVG to a query without turning the query into an aggregate query. You won't need GROUP BY, and you won't lose any detail.

CHAPTER 3

Summarizing with Window Aggregates

In 2005, Microsoft introduced another type of window function to T-SQL, the window aggregates. By adding an OVER clause to an aggregate function, you can avoid the rules you must normally follow. When writing aggregate queries, you lose the details that are not included in the GROUP BY clause. Starting with SQL Server 2005, you can eliminate that restriction by adding the OVER clause. By adding OVER, you may also eliminate the GROUP BY and HAVING clauses. You can also add window aggregate functions to aggregate queries to return summary values at different levels of aggregation.

In this chapter, you will learn how to add aggregate functions by way of window functions to non-aggregate queries. You will also learn to add window aggregate functions to aggregate queries but with different levels of aggregation by way of the OVER clause. You will finish up the chapter by taking a look at some real-world problems.

Using Window Aggregates

Window aggregates are those favorite aggregate functions that you use every day, like SUM and AVG, with the addition of the OVER clause. So far, you have seen the OVER clause used with LAG and the ranking functions. In those situations, an ORDER BY component is required. The ORDER BY component *is not supported* with SQL Server 2005's window aggregate functionality. Chapter 4 covers a 2012 enhancement that does use ORDER BY, but you must learn about the 2005 feature first.

Although the ORDER BY component is not supported in the OVER clause for window aggregates, all window functions support PARTITION BY, and window aggregates are no exception. When leaving out PARTITION BY, you will have an empty OVER clause,

43

© Kathi Kellenberger, Clayton Groom, and Ed Pollack 2019
K. Kellenberger et al., *Expert T-SQL Window Functions in SQL Server 2019*,
https://doi.org/10.1007/978-1-4842-5197-3_3

and the function is applied to the entire set of results, for example, a grand total or overall average. When including PARTITION BY, the function is applied to the individual partitions, for example, subtotals. Here is the syntax:

```
<AggregateFunction>(<col1>) OVER([PARTITION BY <col2>[,<col3>,...<colN>])
```

The built-in aggregate functions that may be used as a window aggregate are listed in Table 3-1.

Table 3-1. *The List of Window Aggregate Functions*

Aggregate Function	Definition
AVG	Calculates the average over the group.
CHECKSUM_AGG	Calculates the checksum over the group. This is often used to detect changes in the data.
COUNT	Used to get a count of the rows or a count of non-null values of a column.
COUNT_BIG	Works like COUNT but returns a big integer.
MAX	Returns the highest value in the set.
MIN	Returns the lowest value in the set.
STDEV	Calculates the standard deviation over the group.
STDEVP	Calculates the standard deviation for the population over the group.
SUM	Adds up the values over the group.
VAR	Returns the statistical variance over the group.
VARP	Returns the statistical variance for the population over the group.

If you review the aggregate functions supported in SQL Server 2019, you'll see three that are not included in this list: GROUPING, GROUPING_ID, and APPROX_COUNT_DISTINCT. GROUPING and GROUPING_ID are used to identify grouping levels when the more advanced GROUP BY options such as ROLLUP are used. APPOX_COUNT_DISTINCT is new with SQL Server 2019. This new function can be used in the case of large data sets in place of COUNT(DISTINCT) when an approximation is good enough. COUNT(DISTINCT) cannot be used as a window function, so it makes sense that APPROX_COUNT_DISTINCT is not allowed either.

The examples in this chapter will focus on the commonly used functions AVG, SUM, MIN, MAX, and COUNT. Listing 3-1 shows some examples of window aggregates.

Listing 3-1. Using Window Aggregates

```
--3.1.1 Window aggregate examples
SELECT CustomerID, SalesOrderID,
    CAST(MIN(OrderDate) OVER() AS DATE) AS FirstOrderDate,
    CAST(MAX(OrderDate) OVER() AS DATE) AS LastOrderDate,
    COUNT(*) OVER() OrderCount,
    FORMAT(SUM(TotalDue) OVER(),'C') TotalAmount
FROM Sales.SalesOrderHeader
ORDER BY CustomerID, SalesOrderID;

--3.1.2 Use PARTITION BY
SELECT CustomerID, SalesOrderID,
    CAST(MIN(OrderDate) OVER(PARTITION BY CustomerID) AS DATE)
        AS FirstOrderDate,
    CAST(MAX(OrderDate) OVER(PARTITION BY CustomerID) AS DATE)
        AS LastOrderDate,
    COUNT(*) OVER(PARTITION BY CustomerID) OrderCount,
    FORMAT(SUM(TotalDue) OVER(PARTITION BY CustomerID),'C') AS TotalAmount
FROM Sales.SalesOrderHeader
ORDER BY CustomerID, SalesOrderID;
```

Figure 3-1 shows the partial results. The first thing to notice about the examples is that there is no GROUP BY clause in either of the queries. Adding a window aggregate expression to an otherwise non-aggregate query does not change the query to an aggregate query. These queries show details of each row along with summary values.

	CustomerID	SalesOrderID	FirstOrderDate	LastOrderDate	OrderCount	TotalAmount
1	11000	43793	2011-05-31	2014-06-30	31465	$123,216,786.12
2	11000	51522	2011-05-31	2014-06-30	31465	$123,216,786.12
3	11000	57418	2011-05-31	2014-06-30	31465	$123,216,786.12
4	11001	43767	2011-05-31	2014-06-30	31465	$123,216,786.12
5	11001	51493	2011-05-31	2014-06-30	31465	$123,216,786.12
6	11001	72773	2011-05-31	2014-06-30	31465	$123,216,786.12

	CustomerID	SalesOrderID	FirstOrderDate	LastOrderDate	OrderCount	TotalAmount
1	11000	43793	2011-06-21	2013-10-03	3	$9,115.13
2	11000	51522	2011-06-21	2013-10-03	3	$9,115.13
3	11000	57418	2011-06-21	2013-10-03	3	$9,115.13
4	11001	43767	2011-06-17	2014-05-12	3	$7,054.19
5	11001	51493	2011-06-17	2014-05-12	3	$7,054.19
6	11001	72773	2011-06-17	2014-05-12	3	$7,054.19

Figure 3-1. *Partial results of using window aggregates*

Query 1 uses the empty OVER clause. This means that the calculations are performed over the entire set of results. The FirstOrderDate is the earliest OrderDate in the data, and the LastOrderDate is the latest OrderDate in the data. The OrderCount is the overall count and the TotalAmount is the grand total of all rows. Query 2 includes a PARTITION BY on CustomerID in each OVER clause. Notice in the results that the values for Query 2 are specific for each customer.

In the previous example, the OVER clause was identical within each query. You may have different OVER clauses within a query. Listing 3-2 has two window aggregate functions in one query with different OVER clauses.

Listing 3-2. Using Different OVER Clauses

```
--3.2.1 Use different OVER clauses
SELECT CustomerID, SalesOrderID, FORMAT(TotalDue,'c') AS TotalDue,
    FORMAT(SUM(TotalDue) OVER(PARTITION BY CustomerID),'c') AS
    CustomerSales,
    FORMAT(SUM(TotalDue) OVER(),'c') AS TotalSales
FROM Sales.SalesOrderHeader
WHERE OrderDate >= '2013-01-01' AND OrderDate < '2014-01-01'
ORDER BY CustomerID, SalesOrderID;
```

Figure 3-2 shows the partial results. This query returns the total for each customer and the overall total.

	CustomerID	SalesOrderID	TotalDue	CustomerSales	TotalSales
1	11000	51522	$2,587.88	$5,358.15	$48,965,887.96
2	11000	57418	$2,770.27	$5,358.15	$48,965,887.96
3	11001	51493	$2,674.02	$2,674.02	$48,965,887.96
4	11002	51238	$2,535.96	$5,209.03	$48,965,887.96
5	11002	53237	$2,673.06	$5,209.03	$48,965,887.96
6	11003	51315	$2,562.45	$5,236.93	$48,965,887.96

Figure 3-2. *The partial results of using different OVER clauses*

Another thing to notice in the previous examples is that some of the window aggregate functions are nested inside the CAST or FORMAT function. The window functions may also operate on columns, more complex expressions, or subqueries just like regular aggregate functions. Listing 3-3 shows an example.

Listing 3-3. Using Window Functions in Expressions

```
--3-3-1 Using window functions in expressions
SELECT CustomerID, SalesOrderID,
    CAST(OrderDate AS Date) AS OrderDate,
    MIN(SalesOrderID/CustomerID)
        OVER(PARTITION BY CustomerID) AS Expr1,
    CAST(MIN(DATEADD(d,1,OrderDate)) OVER() AS DATE) AS Expr2,
    AVG((SELECT COUNT(*)
        FROM Sales.SalesOrderDetail AS SOD
        WHERE SalesOrderID = SOH.SalesOrderID)) OVER() AS Expr3
FROM Sales.SalesOrderHeader AS SOH;
```

The partial results can be seen in Figure 3-3. Expr1 is the quotient of the SalesOrderID divided by the CustomerID. Expr2 nests the DATEADD function inside the MIN function which is nested inside the CAST function. Expr3 applies the AVG function to a subquery and returns the average number of detail rows.

	CustomerID	SalesOrderID	OrderDate	Expr1	Expr2	Expr3
1	11000	43793	2011-06-21	3	2011-06-01	3
2	11000	51522	2013-06-20	3	2011-06-01	3
3	11000	57418	2013-10-03	3	2011-06-01	3
4	11007	54705	2013-08-19	3	2011-06-01	3
5	11007	43743	2011-06-11	3	2011-06-01	3
6	11007	51581	2013-06-23	3	2011-06-01	3
7	11009	43837	2011-06-29	3	2011-06-01	3

Figure 3-3. *The partial results of nesting functions*

You can see that it is easy to add a window aggregate function to any non-aggregate query. Be sure to follow the rules on data types; for example, you can't calculate a sum on character data. You will not use an ORDER BY for this functionality and the PARTITION BY expression is used if you wish to apply the calculations over rows divided into subsets.

A very nonintuitive use of window aggregates is using them within an aggregate query.

Adding Window Aggregates to Aggregate Queries

The first time I added a window aggregate to an aggregate query, I was surprised that it didn't work and more surprised at the error message. Listing 3-4 shows an example.

Listing 3-4. Adding a Window Aggregate to an Aggregate Query

```
--3-4.1 Add a window aggregate to an aggregate query
SELECT CustomerID, SUM(TotalDue) AS CustomerTotal,
    SUM(TotalDue) OVER() AS GrandTotal
FROM Sales.SalesOrderHeader
GROUP BY CustomerID;
```

Figure 3-4 shows the error message.

```
Messages
Msg 8120, Level 16, State 1, Line 2
Column 'Sales.SalesOrderHeader.TotalDue' is invalid
in the select list because it is not contained in either
an aggregate function or the GROUP BY clause.
```

Figure 3-4. *The error message from adding a window aggregate to an*
aggregate query

Obviously, the TotalDue column *is contained* in an aggregate expression, and adding
it to the GROUP BY is certainly not the solution. To understand what is going on here,
you must think about the window that the window aggregate is operating on. The set
of rows in the window is created after GROUP BY operation. The window contains any
expression listed in the GROUP BY clause plus any aggregate expressions. Any expression
contained in any part of a window function must follow the same rules as the SELECT
list. This means that adding CustomerID as the argument of the window function or
as a PARTITION BY column is fine because CustomerID is part of the GROUP BY. To use
TotalDue in any role of the window aggregate expression, it must be aggregated first.
Listing 3-5 shows the correct solution.

Listing 3-5. How to Add a Window Aggregate to an Aggregate Query

```
--3-5.1 How to add a window aggregate to an aggregate query
SELECT CustomerID, SUM(TotalDue) AS CustomerTotal,
    SUM(SUM(TotalDue)) OVER() AS GrandTotal
FROM Sales.SalesOrderHeader
GROUP BY CustomerID;
```

The syntax may look unusual because you cannot nest aggregate functions, but the
window function must be applied to the sum of TotalDue, not just TotalDue. Figure 3-5
shows the partial results and proves that this works.

	CustomerID	CustomerTotal	GrandTotal
1	14324	5659.1783	123216786.1159
2	22814	5.514	123216786.1159
3	11407	59.659	123216786.1159
4	28387	645.2869	123216786.1159
5	19897	659.6408	123216786.1159
6	15675	7963.05	123216786.1159
7	24165	3366.7583	123216786.1159
8	27036	8.0444	123216786.1159

Figure 3-5. *Partial results of adding a window aggregate to an aggregate query*

Another way to do this that is much more intuitive is by separating the window aggregate into a CTE or use another method to separate the logic. Listing 3-6 shows how to do this.

Listing 3-6. Using a CTE instead of nesting

```
--3.6.1 Using a CTE
WITH SALES AS (
    SELECT CustomerID, SUM(TotalDue) AS CustomerTotal
    FROM Sales.SalesOrderHeader
    GROUP BY CustomerID)
SELECT CustomerID, CustomerTotal,
    SUM(CustomerTotal) OVER() AS GrandTotal
FROM Sales;
```

The results are the same as Figure 3-5. Inside the CTE, the query is grouped by CustomerID. A SUM for each customer is calculated, CustomerTotal. In the outer query, the window aggregate is applied to CustomerTotal. The window aggregate is still being applied to the aggregate expression, but the logic is just separated so it's easier to understand. There is no advantage in writing the query this way except to add clarity.

Listing 3-7 has another interesting example involving multiple expressions in the GROUP BY clause.

Listing 3-7. Adding a Window Aggregate to a Query with Multiple Expressions in the GROUP BY Clause

```
--3-7.1 Window aggregate to multiple group by
SELECT YEAR(OrderDate) AS OrderYear,
    CustomerID, SUM(TotalDue) AS CustTotalForYear,
    SUM(SUM(TotalDue)) OVER(PARTITION BY CustomerID) AS CustomerTotal
FROM Sales.SalesOrderHeader
GROUP BY CustomerID, YEAR(OrderDate)
ORDER BY CustomerID, OrderYear;
```

The partial results are shown in Figure 3-6. The GROUP BY clause lists the column CustomerID and the expression YEAR(OrderDate). Before the window aggregate is applied, the results contain one row for each customer per year. The CustTotalForYear is a normal aggregate expression. The final expression is a window aggregate with a PARTITION BY expression on CustomerID, so CustomerTotal is the overall subtotal for the customer. The point of this example is that you can use window aggregate functions to return values at different levels of aggregation.

	OrderYear	CustomerID	CustTotalForYear	CustomerTotal
1	2011	11000	3756.989	9115.1341
2	2013	11000	5358.1451	9115.1341
3	2011	11001	3729.364	7054.1875
4	2013	11001	2674.0227	7054.1875
5	2014	11001	650.8008	7054.1875
6	2011	11002	3756.989	8966.0143
7	2013	11002	5209.0253	8966.0143
8	2011	11003	3756.989	8993.9155

Figure 3-6. *Using a window aggregate with multiple expressions in the GROUP BY*

Inside the window for a window function within an aggregate query, the rows have been filtered and grouped. The list of columns available for use with the window function is restricted by the GROUP BY. This is the default window; you can partition it, but you cannot include anything outside it. You can go smaller but not bigger. You could base the PARTITION BY expression on the entire set of results (empty OVER clause), by CustomerID, or by YEAR(OrderYear) without error. You wouldn't use a combination of CustomerID and YEAR(OrderYear) because that matches the GROUP BY.

The rules for adding a window aggregate to an aggregate query apply to all of the window functions. Always keep in mind that the GROUP BY and HAVING clauses operate first. The results of the FROM, WHERE, GROUP BY, and HAVING clauses determine the rows and columns in the base window and the granularity. Any column used anywhere in the window function must be one of the GROUP BY columns or aggregated inside the window function.

To avoid confusion, do the first aggregation in a CTE. Then, in the outer query, apply the window function.

Using Window Aggregates to Solve Common Queries

It is very easy to add a window aggregate to a complex non-aggregated query. To do the same thing with other methods could double the size of the query.

The Percent of Sales Problem

This particular example can be applied to many situations. You can perform a calculation, such as a percentage, using a window aggregate. Listing 3-8 demonstrates how to display the details along with a percent of sales.

Listing 3-8. Using a Window Function to Display Percent of Sales

```
--3-8.1 Calculate the percent of sales
SELECT P.ProductID,
    FORMAT(SUM(OrderQty * UnitPrice),'C') AS ProductSales,
    FORMAT(SUM(SUM(OrderQty * UnitPrice)) OVER(),'C') AS TotalSales,
    FORMAT(SUM(OrderQty * UnitPrice)/
        SUM(SUM(OrderQty * UnitPrice)) OVER(), 'P') AS PercentOfSales
FROM Sales.SalesOrderDetail AS SOD
JOIN Production.Product AS P ON SOD.ProductID = P.ProductID
```

```
JOIN Production.ProductSubcategory AS SUB ON P.ProductSubcategoryID
    = SUB.ProductSubcategoryID
JOIN Production.ProductCategory AS CAT ON SUB.ProductCategoryID
    = CAT.ProductCategoryID
WHERE CAT.Name = 'Bikes'
GROUP BY P.ProductID
ORDER BY PercentOfSales DESC;
```

Figure 3-7 shows the partial results. This is an aggregate query, so the columns used in any role inside the window aggregate must be a GROUP BY column or aggregated. The empty OVER clause is used to calculate TotalSales. The sum by ProductID is divided by the sales over the entire result set and formatted to give the percentage of sales for each bike model.

	ProductID	ProductSales	TotalSales	PercentOfSales
1	782	$4,406,151.27	$95,145,813.35	4.63 %
2	783	$4,014,067.80	$95,145,813.35	4.21 %
3	779	$3,696,486.47	$95,145,813.35	3.88 %
4	780	$3,441,292.54	$95,145,813.35	3.61 %
5	781	$3,436,090.79	$95,145,813.35	3.61 %
6	784	$3,311,098.44	$95,145,813.35	3.48 %
7	793	$2,518,299.76	$95,145,813.35	2.64 %
8	794	$2,348,246.09	$95,145,813.35	2.46 %

Figure 3-7. *The percent of sales by ProductID*

The Partitioned Table Problem

One of my favorite examples involves looking at the metadata of table partitions. Table partitions have nothing to do with PARTITION BY; it's a feature that makes data management in large databases easier. Since no tables in the AdventureWorks database are partitioned, run Listing 3-9 to create a partitioned table. At one time, you needed Enterprise Edition to run this feature. Microsoft ported the feature to all editions starting with 2016 SP 1.

Listing 3-9. Creating a Partitioned Table

```
--3-9.1 Create the partition function
CREATE PARTITION FUNCTION testFunction (DATE)
AS RANGE RIGHT
FOR VALUES ('2011-01-01','2012-01-01','2013-01-01','2014-01-01');
GO

--3-9.2 Create the partition scheme
CREATE PARTITION SCHEME testScheme
AS PARTITION testFunction ALL TO ('Primary');
GO

--3-9.3 Create a partitioned table
CREATE TABLE dbo.Orders(CustomerID INT, SalesOrderID INT,
    OrderDate DATE, TotalDue MONEY)
ON testScheme(OrderDate);
GO

--3-9.4 Populate the table
INSERT INTO dbo.Orders(customerID, SalesOrderID,
    OrderDate, TotalDue)
SELECT CustomerID, SalesOrderID,
    OrderDate, TotalDue
FROM Sales.SalesOrderHeader;
GO

--3-9.5 Create another partitioned table
CREATE TABLE dbo.Customer (CustomerID INT, ModifiedDate DATE)
ON testScheme(ModifiedDate);
GO

--3-9.6 Populate the table
INSERT INTO dbo.Customer(CustomerID, ModifiedDate)
SELECT CustomerID, ModifiedDate
FROM Sales.Customer;
```

When a table is partitioned, you write queries to retrieve the data in the same way that you always do even though the table is divided up under the covers. If you wish to learn more about table partitioning, be sure to review SQL Server's documentation on the subject since it is out of scope for this book.

A few years ago, my colleague sent me a query and asked for some help. He wanted to see what percentage of rows was found in each partition for a partitioned table. Listing 3-10 shows the query that he sent to me and the solution that I came up with.

Listing 3-10. The Table Partition Question and Solution

```
--3-10.1 The query from my colleague
SELECT OBJECT_NAME(p.OBJECT_ID) TableName,
    ps.partition_number, ps.Row_count
FROM sys.data_spaces  d
JOIN sys.indexes i
JOIN (SELECT DISTINCT OBJECT_ID
      FROM sys.partitions
      WHERE partition_number > 1) p
ON i.OBJECT_ID = p.OBJECT_ID
ON d.data_space_id = i.data_space_id
JOIN sys.dm_db_partition_stats ps
ON i.OBJECT_ID = ps.OBJECT_ID and i.index_id = ps.index_id
WHERE i.index_id < 2;

--3-10.2 The solution to find the percent of rows by table
SELECT OBJECT_NAME(p.OBJECT_ID) TableName,
    ps.partition_number, ps.Row_count,
    --My solution starts here
    FORMAT(ps.row_count * 1.0 /
        SUM(ps.row_count) OVER(PARTITION BY p.OBJECT_ID),'p')
        As PercentOfRows
    --and ends here
FROM sys.data_spaces  d
JOIN sys.indexes i
JOIN (SELECT DISTINCT OBJECT_ID
      FROM sys.partitions
      WHERE partition_number > 1) p
```

```
ON i.OBJECT_ID = p.OBJECT_ID
ON d.data_space_id = i.data_space_id
JOIN sys.dm_db_partition_stats ps
ON i.OBJECT_ID = ps.OBJECT_ID and i.index_id = ps.index_id
WHERE i.index_id < 2;
```

Figure 3-8 shows the results of Query 2. The original query, Query 1, contains all of the columns in the results except for the PercentOfRows column. Hopefully, you agree that the original query is quite complex. The desired solution can be found in Query 2. The Row_count column is divided by the sum of the Row_count partitioned by OBJECT_ID. The partition allows the result to be specific to each table. The answer is also multiplied by 1.0 to eliminate integer division. It has also been formatted for readability. To accomplish the same thing using older methods would be much more difficult to write.

	TableName	partition_number	row_count	PercentOfRows
1	Orders	1	0	0.00 %
2	Orders	2	1607	5.11 %
3	Orders	3	3915	12.44 %
4	Orders	4	14182	45.07 %
5	Orders	5	11761	37.38 %
6	Customer	1	0	0.00 %
7	Customer	2	0	0.00 %
8	Customer	3	0	0.00 %
9	Customer	4	0	0.00 %
10	Customer	5	19820	100.00 %

Figure 3-8. The solution to the table partition problem

To clean up the database objects created in this section, run Listing 3-11.

Listing 3-11. Cleaning Up Database Objects

```
--3-11 Drop objects created in this section
DROP TABLE dbo.Customer;
DROP TABLE dbo.Orders;
DROP PARTITION SCHEME testScheme;
DROP PARTITION FUNCTION testFunction;
```

Whenever you need to use one of the aggregate functions to summarize at a different level than the query's results, think about using a window aggregate.

Creating Custom Window Aggregate Functions

Starting with SQL Server 2005, you can create custom aggregate functions with a .NET language using CLR (Common Language Runtime) integration. Surprisingly, these functions also work as window aggregate functions. Creating a C# DLL is beyond the scope of this BOOK, but the code download for this chapter includes a C# program for such a function. If you would like to learn how to create your own custom function, you can use this project as a model. For more information on creating the custom aggregates, search the SQL Server documentation for "CLR User-Defined Aggregates."

The project contains a DLL file in the chapter's code folder. Copy this file to a location that SQL Server can see such as the C:\Custom folder. You will need to modify the command in Listing 3-12 if you have copied the file to a different location. CLR integration must be enabled as well, so be sure to do this on a local instance of SQL Server, or at least an instance where you are allowed to change this setting. Run Listing 3-12 to set up the custom window aggregate function. Note that the CLR strict security feature was added with SQL Server 2017 but is also available with some updates to SQL Server 2016. If you have a lower version of SLQ Server, comment out the 3-12.2 section of the code.

Listing 3-12. Setting Up a Custom Window Aggregate Function

```
--3-12.1 Enable CRL
EXEC sp_configure 'clr_enabled', 1;
GO
RECONFIGURE;
GO
--3-12.2 Enable an unsigned assembly
```

```
EXEC sp_configure 'show advanced options', 1;
RECONFIGURE;
EXEC sp_configure 'clr strict security',0
GO
RECONFIGURE;
--3-12.3 Register the DLL
CREATE ASSEMBLY CustomAggregate FROM
 'C:\Custom\CustomAggregate.dll' WITH PERMISSION_SET = SAFE;
GO

--3-12.4 Create the function
CREATE Aggregate Median (@Value INT) RETURNS INT
EXTERNAL NAME CustomAggregate.Median;
GO

--3-12.5 Test the function
WITH Orders AS (
    SELECT CustomerID, SUM(OrderQty) AS OrderQty, SOH.SalesOrderID
    FROM Sales.SalesOrderHeader AS SOH
    JOIN Sales.SalesOrderDetail AS SOD
        ON SOH.SalesOrderID = SOD.SalesOrderDetailID
    GROUP BY CustomerID, SOH.SalesOrderID)
SELECT CustomerID, OrderQty, dbo.Median(OrderQty) OVER(PARTITION BY
CustomerID) AS Median
FROM Orders
WHERE CustomerID IN (13011, 13012, 13019);
```

Statement 1 turns on CLR integration for the server. Statement 2 enables the ability to run an unsigned assembly. You should sign any assemblies you plan to use. Statement 3 registers the assembly. Statement 4 enables the new custom function. Query 5 tests the new function, which is called MEDIAN. Figure 3-9 shows the results of using the MEDIAN function. The median returns the middle value when the number of values is odd. It returns the average of the two middle values when the number of values is even. Customer 13011 has three orders. The median of 5, 1, and 3 is 3. Customer 13019 has two orders. The median is 6, halfway between 2 and 10.

	CustomerID	OrderQty	Median
1	13011	5	3
2	13011	1	3
3	13011	3	3
4	13012	3	3
5	13012	1	3
6	13012	24	3
7	13019	10	6
8	13019	2	6

Figure 3-9. *Using the custom MEDIAN function*

If you wish to remove the function and turn off CLR integration, run Listing 3-13.

Listing 3-13. Cleaning Up the Database

```
--3-13.1 Drop the objects
DROP AGGREGATE Median;
DROP ASSEMBLY CustomAggregate;
GO

--3-13.2 Reset CLR integration to the defaults
EXEC sp_configure 'clr_enabled', 0;
GO
RECONFIGURE;
EXEC sp_configure 'clr strict security',1;
GO
```

Summary

Window aggregates make it very easy to add summary calculations to a non-aggregate query or add summaries at different levels of aggregations to aggregate queries. This is very handy when you need to compare the details to an overall total or produce subtotals. If you are really inspired, you can create your own custom window aggregate function.

You now understand how to use all of the window function features released with SQL Server 2005. Chapter 4 demonstrates the first of the features introduced in 2012, the moving and accumulating window aggregates.

CHAPTER 4

Calculating Running and Moving Aggregates

Imagine you have been given the task of writing a T-SQL query with running totals of sales by customer. Maybe your first thought is to use a cursor to do it, or possibly you are familiar with some query techniques like self-joins to accomplish the task. If you are running SQL Server 2012 or later, you are in luck! Window functions make it easy to calculate running totals, moving averages, and more.

In this chapter, you will learn how adding an ORDER BY clause to a windows aggregate expression changes everything! You will learn how to add calculations for running and moving aggregates, something often required in business reports and dashboards.

Adding ORDER BY to Window Aggregates

You learned how to use window aggregates to add summaries to queries without grouping in Chapter 3. The 2005 window aggregate functionality does not support the ORDER BY component in the OVER clause. Starting with SQL Server 2012, you can add an ORDER BY to a window aggregate to calculate running totals. To differentiate between this functionality and the 2005 functionality, this book will call the 2012 functionality *accumulating window aggregates*. When adding the ORDER BY, the window changes. Each row has a different set of rows, or window, to operate on. The window is based on the ORDER BY expression. By default, the window consists of the first row in the results and includes all the subsequent rows up to the current row. Figure 4-1 demonstrates how the windows work when partitioned by CustomerID.

© Kathi Kellenberger, Clayton Groom, and Ed Pollack 2019
K. Kellenberger et al., *Expert T-SQL Window Functions in SQL Server 2019*,
https://doi.org/10.1007/978-1-4842-5197-3_4

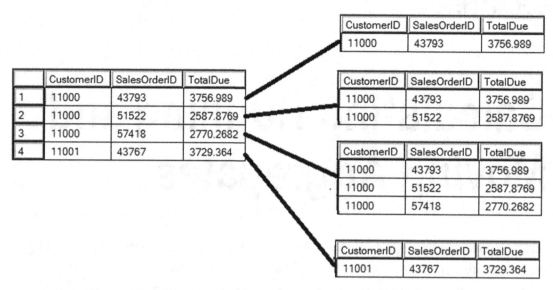

Figure 4-1. *Each row has a different window*

In the examples leading up to this chapter, the actual rows making up the windows were determined by the PARTITION BY expressions. In the case of accumulating aggregates, the PARTITION BY, ORDER BY, and a *frame* define which rows end up in the window. A frame can be used to more finely define the window. The example in this section uses the default frame. You will learn more about frames in the "Calculating Moving Totals and Averages" section in this chapter and even more in Chapter 5. Here is the syntax:

```
<AggregateFunction>(<col1>) OVER([PARTITION BY <expression>]
    ORDER BY <expression> [Frame definition])
```

Listing 4-1 demonstrates how to use accumulating window aggregates to calculate running totals.

Listing 4-1. Calculating Running Totals

```
--4-1.1 A running total
SELECT CustomerID, SalesOrderID, CAST(OrderDate AS DATE) AS OrderDate,
    TotalDue, SUM(TotalDue) OVER(PARTITION BY CustomerID
        ORDER BY SalesOrderID) AS RunningTotal
FROM Sales.SalesOrderHeader;
```

Figure 4-2 shows the partial results. The `RunningTotal` column values increase until reaching a different `CustomerID`. At that point, the totals start over.

	CustomerID	SalesOrderID	OrderDate	TotalDue	RunningTotal
1	11000	43793	2011-06-21	3756.989	3756.989
2	11000	51522	2013-06-20	2587.8769	6344.8659
3	11000	57418	2013-10-03	2770.2682	9115.1341
4	11001	43767	2011-06-17	3729.364	3729.364
5	11001	51493	2013-06-18	2674.0227	6403.3867
6	11001	72773	2014-05-12	650.8008	7054.1875
7	11002	43736	2011-06-09	3756.989	3756.989

Figure 4-2. *Partial results of calculating running totals with accumulating aggregates*

The `OVER` clause in the example shown in Listing 4-1 uses the default frame which is part of the `OVER` clause. Chapter 5 covers framing in depth, but for now you'll learn a bit about it in the next section. By altering the frame, you can calculate moving aggregates.

Calculating Moving Totals and Averages

Moving totals and averages are very popular business and economic metrics. Developers may be asked to provide reports with these calculations over 3 months or over 12 months, for example. By default, the window for accumulating window aggregates keeps growing within the partition, but for moving aggregates, you want the window size to stay the same. You can accomplish this by adding a frame definition. Here is the syntax for accumulating window aggregates including the frame for a moving aggregate. Chapter 5 covers framing extensively, so for now just copy the code in the examples.

```
<AggregateFunction>(<col1>) OVER([PARTITION BY <expression>]]
    ORDER BY <expression>
    [ROWS BETWEEN <number> PRECEDING AND CURRENT ROW])
```

The window is different for each row. Figure 4-3 demonstrates how the window works for a moving aggregate.

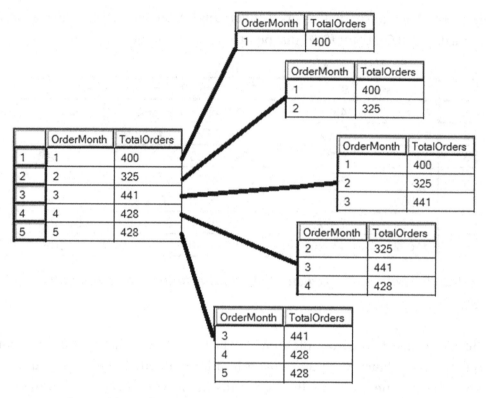

Figure 4-3. *The windows for a moving aggregate over 3 months*

Run Listing 4-2 to see an example.

Listing 4-2. Calculating Moving Averages and Sums

```
--4-2.1 Three month sum and average for products qty sold
SELECT MONTH(SOH.OrderDate) AS OrderMonth, SOD.ProductID, SUM(SOD.OrderQty)
AS QtySold,
    SUM(SUM(SOD.OrderQty))
    OVER(PARTITION BY SOD.ProductID ORDER BY MONTH(SOH.OrderDate)
    ROWS BETWEEN 2 PRECEDING AND CURRENT ROW) AS ThreeMonthSum,
    AVG(SUM(SOD.OrderQty))
    OVER(PARTITION BY SOD.ProductID ORDER BY MONTH(SOH.OrderDate)
    ROWS BETWEEN 2 PRECEDING AND CURRENT ROW) AS ThreeMonthAvg
FROM Sales.SalesOrderHeader AS SOH
JOIN Sales.SalesOrderDetail AS SOD ON SOH.SalesOrderID = SOD.SalesOrderID
```

```
JOIN Production.Product AS P ON SOD.ProductID = P.ProductID
WHERE OrderDate >= '2013-01-01' AND OrderDate < '2014-01-01'
GROUP BY MONTH(SOH.OrderDate), SOD.ProductID;
```

The query is filtered for orders placed in 2013 and aggregated to the month and
ProductID. Figure 4-4 shows the partial results, one year's sales of product 707. Notice
that the window function in each case is applied to an aggregate, the sum of OrderQty.
When using a window function in an aggregate query, any columns used in the function
or the OVER clause follow the same rules as the SELECT list. See the "Adding Window
Aggregates to Aggregate Queries" section in Chapter 3 for more information. By adding
ORDER BY and the ROWS expression (frame) to the OVER clause, the window moves forward
and includes at most three rows each time.

	OrderMonth	ProductID	QtySold	ThreeMonthSum	ThreeMonthAvg
1	1	707	45	45	45
2	2	707	111	156	78
3	3	707	146	302	100
4	4	707	146	403	134
5	5	707	226	518	172
6	6	707	285	657	219
7	7	707	448	959	319
8	8	707	314	1047	349
9	9	707	320	1082	360
10	10	707	345	979	326
11	11	707	296	961	320
12	12	707	258	899	299

Figure 4-4. Partial results of calculating moving aggregates

Most of the time, the requirements for three-month calculations specify that the
values should be NULL if there are not three months to average, but the functions will
just add up whatever is available. For example, the three-month sums and averages for
January and February should be NULL. Starting in March, the three months are available,
so the total is returned. To accomplish this, you'll have to check for the number of
months. Listing 4-3 shows one way to do this.

Listing 4-3. Display NULL When Not Enough Rows

```
--4-3.1 Display NULL when less than
SELECT MONTH(SOH.OrderDate) AS OrderMonth, SOD.ProductID,
    SUM(SOD.OrderQty) AS QtySold,
    CASE WHEN ROW_NUMBER() OVER(PARTITION BY SOD.ProductID
        ORDER BY MONTH(SOH.OrderDate)) < 3 THEN NULL
    ELSE  SUM(SUM(SOD.OrderQty)) OVER(PARTITION BY SOD.ProductID
        ORDER BY MONTH(SOH.OrderDate)
        ROWS BETWEEN 2 PRECEDING AND CURRENT ROW) END AS ThreeMonthSum,
    CASE WHEN ROW_NUMBER() OVER(PARTITION BY SOD.ProductID
        ORDER BY MONTH(SOH.OrderDate)) < 3 THEN NULL
      ELSE AVG(SUM(SOD.OrderQty))
        OVER(PARTITION BY SOD.ProductID ORDER BY MONTH(SOH.OrderDate)
        ROWS BETWEEN 2 PRECEDING AND CURRENT ROW) END AS ThreeMonthAvg
FROM Sales.SalesOrderHeader AS SOH
JOIN Sales.SalesOrderDetail AS SOD ON SOH.SalesOrderID = SOD.SalesOrderID
JOIN Production.Product AS P ON SOD.ProductID = P.ProductID
WHERE OrderDate >= '2013-01-01' AND OrderDate < '2014-01-01'
GROUP BY MONTH(SOH.OrderDate), SOD.ProductID;
```

Figure 4-5 shows the partial results, one year's worth of sales for ProductID 707. By using a CASE statement to check the ROW_NUMBER, NULL is returned when less than three rows are available.

	OrderMonth	ProductID	QtySold	ThreeMonthSum	ThreeMonthAvg
1	1	707	45	NULL	NULL
2	2	707	111	NULL	NULL
3	3	707	146	302	100
4	4	707	146	403	134
5	5	707	226	518	172
6	6	707	285	657	219
7	7	707	448	959	319
8	8	707	314	1047	349
9	9	707	320	1082	360
10	10	707	345	979	326
11	11	707	296	961	320
12	12	707	258	899	299

Figure 4-5. *Return NULL when less than three rows are available*

Solving Queries Using Accumulating Aggregates

Creating running and moving aggregates is very easy! You will learn how to take advantage of the frame component of the OVER clause in Chapter 5 to make sure you get the results you expect. In Chapter 8, the performance of framing is covered, which is also important. Unlike the ranking functions, calculating a running or moving aggregate may be the solution not just a step along the way to the solution. The following section shows how to use accumulating window functions to solve even more interesting problems.

The Last Good Value Problem

I ran across this problem in a forum, and several people tried to solve it. The best solution was developed by T-SQL guru, Itzik Ben-Gan.

The table for this problem has two columns. The first, ID, is an incrementing integer, the primary key of the table. The second column may contain NULL values. The task is to replace each NULL with the previous non-NULL value. Listing 4-4 creates and populates the table and displays the rows.

Listing 4-4. Creating and Populating the Table

```
--4-4.1 Create the table
CREATE TABLE #TheTable(ID INT, Data INT);

--4-4.2 Populate the table
INSERT INTO #TheTable(ID, Data)
VALUES(1,1),(2,1),(3,NULL),
    (4,NULL),(5,6),(6,NULL),
    (7,5),(8,10),(9,13),
    (10,12),(11,NULL);

--4-4.3 Display the results
SELECT * FROM #TheTable;
```

Figure 4-6 shows the raw data in the table. Notice that rows 3, 4, 6, and 11 have NULL in the Data column. The solution will replace the NULL with 1 for rows 3 and 4, with 6 for row 6, and with 12 for row 11.

	ID	Data
1	1	1
2	2	1
3	3	NULL
4	4	NULL
5	5	6
6	6	NULL
7	7	5
8	8	10
9	9	13
10	10	12
11	11	NULL

Figure 4-6. *The data for the last good value problem*

I found Itzik's solution to be quite elegant and brilliant. It takes advantage of the fact that you can use any of the aggregate functions as accumulating window aggregates, not just SUM and AVG. Take a look at row 4. The value needed to replace the NULL is the Data value from row 2. The ID of row 2 is also the maximum ID for the rows leading up to row 4 that are not NULL in the Data column. A window that starts at row 1 of a partition and goes up to the current row is the same window that you need for a running total! You can take advantage of this fact to find the maximum ID leading up to the current row where the Data value is not NULL. Listing 4-5 shows step 1 of this solution.

Listing 4-5. Step 1 of the Solution

```
--4-5.1 Find the max non-null row
SELECT ID, Data,
    MAX(CASE WHEN Data IS NOT NULL THEN ID END)
    OVER(ORDER BY ID) AS MaxRowID
FROM #TheTable;
```

Figure 4-7 shows the results so far. The MaxRowID column is the ID from the row that contains the Data value that each row needs. The MAX function finds the largest ID value for rows that have a non-NULL Data value up to the current row.

	ID	Data	MaxRowID
1	1	1	1
2	2	1	2
3	3	NULL	2
4	4	NULL	2
5	5	6	5
6	6	NULL	5
7	7	5	7
8	8	10	8
9	9	13	9
10	10	12	10
11	11	NULL	10

Figure 4-7. *The results of step 1*

My first thought is that I could use the MaxRowID column to join the table to itself, but take a look at this data closely. Within each group of rows with the same MaxRowID value, there is one non-NULL Data row, and the rest are NULL. There are three rows where MaxRowID is 2. Only one of those rows has a non-NULL Data value. My next thought is to just group by MaxRowID and use the MAX function on the Data column. The problem is that you would lose the details that you need to see by doing so. But window aggregates let you add an aggregate function without changing the query to an aggregate query. Instead of grouping on MaxRowID, partition on it. Listing 4-6 shows the complete solution.

Listing 4-6. The Complete Solution

```
--4-6.1 The solution
WITH MaxData AS
    (SELECT ID, Data,
        MAX(CASE WHEN Data IS NOT NULL THEN ID END)
        OVER(ORDER BY ID) AS MaxRowID
    FROM #TheTable)
SELECT ID, Data,
    MAX(Data) OVER(PARTITION BY MaxRowID) AS NewData
FROM MaxData;
```

Figure 4-8 shows the results. The first part of the solution is added to a CTE. In the outer query, the MAX function is used to find the maximum Data value, actually the only one that is not NULL, partitioned by the MaxRowID.

	ID	Data	NewData
1	1	1	1
2	2	1	1
3	3	NULL	1
4	4	NULL	1
5	5	6	6
6	6	NULL	6
7	7	5	5
8	8	10	10
9	9	13	13
10	10	12	12
11	11	NULL	12

Figure 4-8. *The complete results of the Last Good Value Problem*

The solution seems quite simple once you see it. Thanks to Itzik Ben-Gan for figuring this out.

The Subscription Problem

In today's world, many of us do not have magazine or newspaper subscriptions, but they were very popular not too long ago. Customers subscribed to the publication and sometimes cancelled at some point. In this problem, you must calculate the number of active subscriptions at the end of each month. There will be cancellation dates past the latest subscription date, and you can ignore those rows.

The most intuitive way to solve this problem is by using a temp table with a row for each month. Loop through each row of the data and add or subtract based on the start and stop dates. Unfortunately, this method runs extremely slow. Using the accumulating aggregate functionality makes this problem easy to solve, and it runs fast!

To get started, create a temp table with some random registration data. Since this is random, your final results will not match mine. This script creates a table holding 100,000 rows, but you can adjust that number if you wish. Listing 4-7 creates and populates the table.

Listing 4-7. Create the Subscription Table

```
--4-7.1 Create the temp table
CREATE TABLE #Registrations(ID INT NOT NULL IDENTITY PRIMARY KEY,
        DateJoined DATE NOT NULL, DateLeft DATE NULL);

--4-7.2 Variables
DECLARE @Rows INT = 10000, @Years INT = 5, @StartDate DATE = '2019-01-01'

--4-7.3 Insert 10,000 rows with five years of possible dates
INSERT INTO #Registrations (DateJoined)
SELECT TOP(@Rows) DATEADD(DAY,CAST(RAND(CHECKSUM(NEWID())) * @Years *
365  as INT) ,@StartDate)
FROM sys.objects a
CROSS JOIN sys.objects b
CROSS JOIN sys.objects c;

--4-7.4 Give cancellation dates to 75% of the subscribers
UPDATE TOP(75) PERCENT #Registrations
SET DateLeft = DATEADD(DAY,CAST(RAND(CHECKSUM(NEWID())) * @Years * 365
as INT),DateJoined)

--4-7.5 The subscription data
SELECT *
FROM #Registrations
ORDER BY DateJoined;
```

The partial results will look something like Figure 4-9.

	ID	DateJoined	DateLeft
1	433	2019-01-01	2022-03-03
2	766	2019-01-01	2023-10-31
3	7895	2019-01-01	NULL
4	8465	2019-01-02	NULL
5	6506	2019-01-02	2020-03-22
6	1901	2019-01-02	2021-10-30
7	2565	2019-01-02	2023-10-29
8	3905	2019-01-02	2021-07-15
9	9302	2019-01-02	NULL
10	9850	2019-01-03	NULL
11	4046	2019-01-03	2021-10-16
12	2783	2019-01-03	2022-07-29

Figure 4-9. The partial subscription data

If you read an article (www.red-gate.com/simple-talk/sql/performance/writing-efficient-sql-set-based-speed-phreakery/) I wrote back in 2009 to solve a similar problem, you'll see that efficient code was also complicated and hard to understand. In the article, I explained a solution by T-SQL guru Peter Larsson that used a temp table, UNPIVOT, and an unsupported "quirky" update. Armed with SQL Server 2012, a solution to this problem is very easy to write, and it performs well. Listing 4-8 shows the solution.

Listing 4-8. Solving the Subscription Problem with SQL Server 2012 Functionality

```
--4-8.1 Solve the subscription problem
WITH NewSubs AS (
    SELECT EOMONTH(DateJoined) AS TheMonth,
        COUNT(DateJoined) AS PeopleJoined
    FROM #Registrations
    GROUP BY EOMONTH(DateJoined)),
```

```
Cancelled AS (
    SELECT EOMONTH(DateLeft) AS TheMonth,
        COUNT(DateLeft) AS PeopleLeft
    FROM #Registrations
    GROUP BY EOMONTH(DateLeft))
SELECT NewSubs.TheMonth AS TheMonth, NewSubs.PeopleJoined,
    Cancelled.PeopleLeft,
    SUM(NewSubs.PeopleJoined - ISNULL(Cancelled.PeopleLeft,0))
    OVER(ORDER BY NewSubs.TheMonth) AS Subscriptions
FROM NewSubs
LEFT JOIN Cancelled ON NewSubs.TheMonth = Cancelled.TheMonth;
```

The partial results are shown in Figure 4-10. The first step is to get a count by month for new subscriptions and cancellations. To do that, the data must be grouped by month. In this case, the EOMONTH function is used, which changes each date to the last day of the month.

	TheMonth	PeopleJoined	PeopleLeft	Subscriptions
1	2019-01-31	154	1	153
2	2019-02-28	155	5	303
3	2019-03-31	158	1	460
4	2019-04-30	178	5	633
5	2019-05-31	165	8	790
6	2019-06-30	169	13	946
7	2019-07-31	183	17	1112
8	2019-08-31	157	22	1247
9	2019-09-30	173	18	1402
10	2019-10-31	178	13	1567
11	2019-11-30	151	25	1693
12	2019-12-31	173	29	1837

Figure 4-10. *Partial results of the Subscription Problem*

The new subscription and cancellation counts are separated into CTEs to get the PeopleJoined and PeopleLeft values, respectively, for each month. The outer query joins the NewSubs CTE to the Cancelled CTE with a LEFT JOIN because there are many months with no cancellations. The sum of PeopleJoined minus PeopleLeft after PeopleLeft is corrected for NULL is calculated as a running total.

The query was very easy to write and runs pretty fast. It ran in less than 100 milliseconds on my Azure virtual machine against 100,000 rows.

Summary

Starting with SQL Server 2012, adding an ORDER BY to the OVER clause changes a window aggregate into an accumulating window aggregate. This lets you easily create running totals plus moving totals and averages. You are not limited to using this functionality for just sums and averages, however. The MAX function was also used to solve a difficult problem.

You were briefly introduced to frames in this chapter when looking at moving sums and averages. Chapter 5 takes a deep look at frames.

CHAPTER 5

Adding Frames to the Window

You have looked through the window and used it to write powerful queries to solve some common problems. You have partitioned it like the smaller panes in a large window. Now you will learn how to create very granular windows, much like stained glass, with the use of frames.

In this chapter, you will learn how framing, where it is supported, is so important for the accuracy of the results. The frame is also important for performance, but you will learn about that in Chapter 8.

Understanding Framing

When the 2012 T-SQL features were first announced back in 2011, I must confess that framing intimidated me a bit. I avoided learning about it as long as I could because I didn't really like the syntax and didn't quite understand what was going on. Luckily, frames are only supported with specific window functions, so they are not used too often. The scariest things in life, like public speaking, often turn out to have the biggest payoffs, and framing in window function expressions is no different. Taking the time to understand framing will really help you get the most from window functions.

With framing, you can specify a window that is smaller than the partition. For example, you may want a window that starts at the first row of the set but stops at the current row. You may want a window that starts just 12 rows before the current row regardless of how many rows are in the partition. With frames, you can define windows that meet these special requirements.

Before you start adding frames to your OVER clauses, you should understand several key terms. Table 5-1 lists the terms and the definitions.

© Kathi Kellenberger, Clayton Groom, and Ed Pollack 2019
K. Kellenberger et al., *Expert T-SQL Window Functions in SQL Server 2019*,
https://doi.org/10.1007/978-1-4842-5197-3_5

Table 5-1. *Key Framing Terms*

Key Term	Definition
ROWS	A physical operator. Looks at the position of the rows.
RANGE	A logical operator, but not fully implemented in the current versions of SQL Server. Looks at the value of an expression instead of the position.
UNBOUNDED PRECEDING	The frame starts at the first row in the set.
UNBOUNDED FOLLOWING	The frame ends at the final row in the set.
N PRECEDING	A physical number of rows before the current row. Supported only with ROWS.
N FOLLOWING	A physical number of rows after the current row. Supported only with ROWS.
CURRENT ROW	The row of the current calculation.

You saw in Chapter 4 that the window for accumulating aggregates is different for every row. If you are calculating a running total, the window for row 1 is row 1. The window for row 2 is rows 1 and 2. The window for row 3 is rows 1 to 3, and so on. In each case, the window begins at the first row of the partition and ends at the current row. Figure 5-1 shows what the frames look like when partitioned by CustomerID. Notice that the window for row 4 is in a new partition, CustomerID 11001, and row 4 is the first row in that partition.

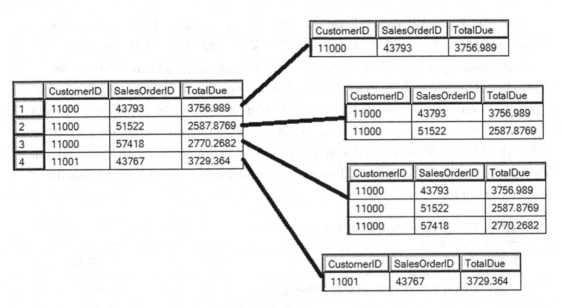

Figure 5-1. *Each row has a different window*

The frame definition consists of the keyword ROWS or RANGE followed by the word BETWEEN. Then you must specify a starting point and ending point. Here is the syntax:

```
ROWS BETWEEN <starting expression> AND <ending expression>
RANGE BETWEEN <starting expression> AND <ending expression>
```

There are two possible frame expressions that will give you an accumulating aggregate, like a running total, starting with the first row of the partition and ending with the current row: ROWS BETWEEN UNBOUNDED PRECEDING AND CURRENT ROW and RANGE BETWEEN UNBOUNDED PRECEDING AND CURRENT ROW. You will learn more about the differences between ROWS and RANGE later in the chapter, but for now, you should understand that RANGE BETWEEN UNBOUNDED PRECEDING AND CURRENT ROW is the default frame where a frame is supported but not specified. That is why you can just add an ORDER BY expression to an OVER clause for SUM and produce a running total. The expressions SUM(TotalDue) OVER(ORDER BY OrderID) and SUM(TotalDue) OVER(ORDER BY OrderID RANGE BETWEEN UNBOUNDED PRECEDING AND CURRENT ROW) are equivalent.

For reasons that you will learn later in the chapter, the preferred frame expression uses ROWS instead of RANGE. You can also use an abbreviated syntax for the running total frame: ROWS UNBOUNDED PRECEDING.

To create a frame that starts at the current row and includes all of the rows to the end of the set, use ROWS BETWEEN CURRENT ROW AND UNBOUNDED FOLLOWING. This will allow you to create a reverse running total. Another way to use a frame is by specifying a number of rows to include in the frame. This syntax can only be used with ROWS. You can specify a number of rows before, after, or before and after the current row. There is also a shortcut for this expression if you intend a number of rows before the current row: ROWS <N> PRECEDING. Imagine that you have a partition consisting of 10 rows, and that the current row is row 5. Table 5-2 lists several frame examples and the rows that the examples refer to.

Table 5-2. *Framing Examples*

Frame	Rows
ROWS BETWEEN 3 PRECEDING AND CURRENT ROW	2–5
ROWS BETWEEN CURRENT ROW AND 4 FOLLOWING	5–9
ROWS BETWEEN 3 PRECEDING AND 4 FOLLOWING	2–9
ROWS I RANGE BETWEEN UNBOUNDED PRECEDING AND CURRENT ROW	1–5
ROWS I RANGE BETWEEN CURRENT ROW AND UNBOUNDED FOLLOWING	5–10

Figure 5-2 illustrates these examples.

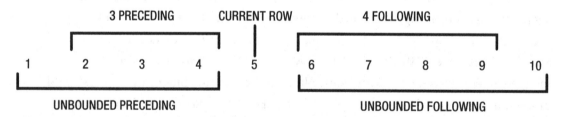

Figure 5-2. *Some framing examples*

The RANGE operator can't be used when specifying a number of rows preceding or following, but it can be used with UNBOUNDED PRECEDING and UNBOUNDED FOLLOWING phrases. It's unlikely anyone will specify RANGE on purpose; they are most likely to leave the frame out and get RANGE by default.

There is functionality in the SQL standards that has been left out of the implementation in T-SQL. This functionality allows you to specify a time period instead of a number of rows. Listing 5-1 is a theoretical query that may be available someday.

Listing 5-1. A Theoretical Query Using Range As It's Intended

```
--5-1.1 A theoretical query
SELECT SUM(TotalDue) OVER(ORDER BY OrderDate
RANGE BETWEEN INTERVAL 5 MONTH PRECEDING and 1 MONTH FOLLOWING
) SixMonthTotal
FROM Sales.SalesOrderHeader;
```

Before learning about the differences between ROWS and RANGE for the currently implemented functionality, review a few examples using frames.

Applying Frames to Running and Moving Aggregates

Frames were first introduced to SQL Server with the 2012 version. They apply to a subset of window functions, the accumulating aggregates you learned about in Chapter 4 and two of the offset functions, FIRST_VALUE and LAST_VALUE. You will learn about offset functions in Chapter 6.

By specifying the frame, you can calculate reverse running totals and moving aggregates. Run Listing 5-2 to see some examples.

Listing 5-2. Using Frames

```
--5-2.1 Running and reverse running totals
SELECT CustomerID, CAST(OrderDate AS DATE) AS OrderDate, SalesOrderID,
TotalDue,
    SUM(TotalDue) OVER(PARTITION BY CustomerID ORDER BY SalesOrderID
    ROWS UNBOUNDED PRECEDING) AS RunningTotal,
    SUM(TotalDue) OVER(PARTITION BY CustomerID ORDER BY SalesOrderID
    ROWS BETWEEN CURRENT ROW AND UNBOUNDED FOLLOWING) AS ReverseTotal
FROM Sales.SalesOrderHeader
ORDER BY CustomerID, SalesOrderID;

--5-2.2 Moving sum and average
SELECT YEAR(OrderDate) AS OrderYear, MONTH(OrderDate) AS OrderMonth,
    COUNT(*) AS OrderCount,
    SUM(COUNT(*)) OVER(ORDER BY YEAR(OrderDate), MONTH(OrderDate)
```

```
      ROWS BETWEEN 2 PRECEDING AND CURRENT ROW) AS ThreeMonthCount,
      AVG(COUNT(*)) OVER(ORDER BY YEAR(OrderDate), MONTH(OrderDate)
      ROWS BETWEEN 2 PRECEDING AND CURRENT ROW) AS ThreeMonthAvg
FROM Sales.SalesOrderHeader
WHERE OrderDate >= '2012-01-01' AND OrderDate < '2013-01-01'
GROUP BY YEAR(OrderDate), MONTH(OrderDate);
```

Figure 5-3 shows the partial results. By specifying that the window should start at the current row and continue to the end of the partition, you can create a reverse running total as in Query 1. By specifying that the window is made up of two rows before the current row and the current row as in Query 2, you create a window that moves.

	CustomerID	OrderDate	SalesOrderID	TotalDue	RunningTotal	ReverseTotal
1	11000	2011-06-21	43793	3756.989	3756.989	9115.1341
2	11000	2013-06-20	51522	2587.8769	6344.8659	5358.1451
3	11000	2013-10-03	57418	2770.2682	9115.1341	2770.2682
4	11001	2011-06-17	43767	3729.364	3729.364	7054.1875
5	11001	2013-06-18	51493	2674.0227	6403.3867	3324.8235
6	11001	2014-05-12	72773	650.8008	7054.1875	650.8008

	OrderYear	OrderMonth	OrderCount	ThreeMonthCount	ThreeMonthAvg
1	2012	1	336	336	336
2	2012	2	219	555	277
3	2012	3	304	859	286
4	2012	4	269	792	264
5	2012	5	293	866	288
6	2012	6	390	952	317

Figure 5-3. *The partial results of using the frame*

You may notice that the calculations using N PRECEDING return values when less than three months of rows is available. To get around this, you can filter out rows that don't qualify. Listing 5-3 shows how you might want to do this.

Listing 5-3. Filter Rows with Less Than Two Preceding Rows

```
--5-3.1 Filter rows with less than 2 preceding rows
WITH Sales AS (
    SELECT YEAR(OrderDate) AS OrderYear, MONTH(OrderDate) AS OrderMonth,
        COUNT(*) AS OrderCount,
        SUM(COUNT(*)) OVER(ORDER BY YEAR(OrderDate), MONTH(OrderDate)
        ROWS BETWEEN 2 PRECEDING AND CURRENT ROW) AS ThreeMonthCount,
        AVG(COUNT(*)) OVER(ORDER BY YEAR(OrderDate), MONTH(OrderDate)
            ROWS BETWEEN 2 PRECEDING AND CURRENT ROW) AS ThreeMonthAvg,
        ROW_NUMBER() OVER(PARTITION BY YEAR(OrderDate)
            ORDER BY MONTH(OrderDate)) AS RowNum
    FROM Sales.SalesOrderHeader
    GROUP BY YEAR(OrderDate), MONTH(OrderDate)
)
SELECT OrderYear, OrderMonth, OrderCount, ThreeMonthCount, ThreeMonthAvg
FROM Sales
WHERE RowNum >= 3;
```

This query includes ROW_NUMBER partitioned on the year so that May and June of 2011 are not returned. Figure 5-4 shows the partial results.

	OrderYear	OrderMonth	OrderCount	ThreeMonthCount	ThreeMonthAvg
1	2011	7	231	415	138
2	2011	8	250	622	207
3	2011	9	157	638	212
4	2011	10	327	734	244
5	2011	11	230	714	238
6	2011	12	228	785	261
7	2012	3	304	859	286
8	2012	4	269	792	264
9	2012	5	293	866	288
10	2012	6	390	952	317

Figure 5-4. *The partial results of filtering out less than rows*

To get the moving aggregates, like the ThreeMonthAvg shown in the previous examples, you must use the frame. If you just want a running total, you may be able to get by leaving it out. The ReverseTotal did require the frame because it starts at the end of the data and ends at the current row. Often when giving a presentation on window functions, someone will mention that changing the ORDER BY expression to descending will give a reverse running total, and they are correct. Listing 5-4 shows an example.

Listing 5-4. Running Totals and Reverse Running Totals Without the Frame

```
--5-4.1 Running and reverse running totals
SELECT CustomerID, CAST(OrderDate AS DATE) AS OrderDate, SalesOrderID,
TotalDue,
    SUM(TotalDue) OVER(PARTITION BY CustomerID ORDER BY SalesOrderID) AS
    RunningTotal,
    SUM(TotalDue) OVER(PARTITION BY CustomerID ORDER BY SalesOrderID DESC
    ) AS ReverseTotal
FROM Sales.SalesOrderHeader
ORDER BY CustomerID, SalesOrderID;
```

The results are the same as that shown in the first query in Figure 5-3. Before SQL Server 2019, I would have warned not to do this because of performance implications. You'll learn more about the performance of differences between ROWS and RANGE in Chapter 8. Until then, you do need to be aware of a critical difference in the logic of these two operators.

Understanding the Logical Difference Between ROWS and RANGE

In Chapter 8, you will see that frames using ROWS have a big performance advantage over RANGE when working in versions of SQL Server before 2019. There is also a logical difference between the two operators. The ROWS operator is a positional operator, while the RANGE operator is a logical one. This is very similar to the difference between ROW_NUMBER and RANK. When there are ties in the ORDER BY expression, RANK will repeat the value, while ROW_NUMBER will return a unique value. If there are ties in the ORDER BY expression of the OVER clause when calculating running totals, ROWS and RANGE will return different results as well. Run Listing 5-5 to see this difference.

Listing 5-5. The Difference Between ROWS and RANGE

```
--5-5.1 Compare the logical difference between ROWS and RANGE
SELECT CustomerID, CAST(OrderDate AS DATE) AS OrderDate, SalesOrderID,
TotalDue,
    SUM(TotalDue) OVER(ORDER BY OrderDate
        ROWS UNBOUNDED PRECEDING) AS RunningTotalRows,
    SUM(TotalDue) OVER(ORDER BY OrderDate
        RANGE UNBOUNDED PRECEDING) AS RunningTotalRange
FROM Sales.SalesOrderHeader
WHERE CustomerID =11300
ORDER BY SalesOrderID;
```

The partial results are shown in Figure 5-5. The ORDER BY expressions in the OVER clauses are both OrderDate, which is not unique. Take a look at rows 7 and 8 where the customer has placed two orders on the same day. The RunningTotalRows values increment as expected, while the RunningTotalRange value is the same for both rows. On row 9, the RunningTotalRange value lines back up again.

	CustomerID	OrderDate	SalesOrderID	TotalDue	RunningTotalRows	RunningTotalRange
1	11300	2013-07-03	52035	45.957	45.957	45.957
2	11300	2013-07-04	52083	35.6694	81.6264	81.6264
3	11300	2013-08-04	53835	101.1959	182.8223	182.8223
4	11300	2013-08-14	54388	82.8529	265.6752	265.6752
5	11300	2013-08-19	54662	8.7848	274.46	274.46
6	11300	2013-09-20	56487	38.664	313.124	313.124
7	11300	2013-10-21	58365	97.7483	410.8723	453.8347
8	11300	2013-10-21	58370	42.9624	453.8347	453.8347
9	11300	2013-11-14	60130	9.934	463.7687	463.7687
10	11300	2013-12-06	61611	66.8194	530.5881	530.5881

Figure 5-5. *Partial results of comparing ROWS to RANGE*

The window for ROWS in this case starts with the first row and includes all rows up to the current row sorted by the ORDER BY. The window for RANGE is all rows starting with the first row and up to any rows with the *same value* as the current row's ORDER BY expression. When the window for row 7 is determined, RANGE looks at not just the position but also the value. The value for the OrderDate for row 8 is the same as the value for row 7, so row 8 is included in the window for row 7.

Just in case you think there is a bug with RANGE, run Listing 5-6, which uses one of the older techniques and returns the identical results to using RANGE.

Listing 5-6. Same Results from Older Technique

```
--5-6.1 Look at the older technique
SELECT CustomerID, CAST(OrderDate AS DATE) AS OrderDate,
    SalesOrderID, TotalDue,
    (SELECT SUM(TotalDue)
    FROM Sales.SalesOrderHeader AS IQ
    WHERE IQ.CustomerID = OQ.CustomerID
        AND IQ.OrderDate <= OQ.OrderDate) AS RunningTotal
FROM Sales.SalesOrderHeader AS OQ
WHERE CustomerID =11300
ORDER BY SalesOrderID;
```

The partial results are shown in Figure 5-6. Take a look at rows 7 and 8. You'll see that because the OrderDate values are the same, the RunningTotal values are the same as well.

	CustomerID	OrderDate	SalesOrderID	TotalDue	RunningTotal
1	11300	2013-07-03	52035	45.957	45.957
2	11300	2013-07-04	52083	35.6694	81.6264
3	11300	2013-08-04	53835	101.1959	182.8223
4	11300	2013-08-14	54388	82.8529	265.6752
5	11300	2013-08-19	54662	8.7848	274.46
6	11300	2013-09-20	56487	38.664	313.124
7	11300	2013-10-21	58365	97.7483	453.8347
8	11300	2013-10-21	58370	42.9624	453.8347
9	11300	2013-11-14	60130	9.934	463.7687
10	11300	2013-12-06	61611	66.8194	530.5881

Figure 5-6. *Partial results of using an older technique to calculate running totals*

If you ensure that the ORDER BY expression is unique, you will get the expected results with both the old method and with a window aggregate using the default frame.

As mentioned previously, the RANGE operator is really meant to work with logical sets such as months or quarters. This functionality has been defined by the ANSI standard but is not implemented at this time in SQL Server. In the meantime, make sure you always specify the frame with ROWS.

Summary

It's easy to write a query that calculates running totals or moving averages. By default, the frame is defined with RANGE, but ROWS is recommended just in case the ORDER BY expression is not unique. In older versions of SQL Server, you will also see a performance boost by using ROWS which you'll learn about in Chapter 8. The frame also allows you to specify a window size that moves down the results for calculations such as three-month averages.

The syntax for the frame is not easy to learn, but there is no shame in looking up the syntax found in this chapter from time to time. Luckily, you do not have to worry about the frame except when using accumulating window aggregates and the functions FIRST_VALUE and LAST_VALUE. You will learn about FIRST_VALUE and LAST_VALUE in the next chapter, Chapter 6.

CHAPTER 6

Taking a Peek at Another Row

Along with accumulating window aggregates, Microsoft added eight new window functions with SQL Server 2012. Four of the functions, which I'll call offset functions in this book, are my favorite T-SQL functions, and they are LAG, LEAD, FIRST_VALUE, and LAST_VALUE. These functions let you include any columns from other rows in your results without a self-join and with fantastic performance.

In this chapter, you will learn how to use LAG, LEAD, FIRST_VALUE, and LAST_VALUE. You will see how easy they are to use. The performance is great, but you'll learn about that in Chapter 8.

Understanding LAG and LEAD

You saw how to use LAG in Chapter 1 to solve the stock market problem. Based on the ORDER BY expression of the OVER clause, you can use LAG to include a column from a row earlier in the results and LEAD to include a column later in the results. Framing is not supported with LAG and LEAD, so you don't have to worry about performance most of the time. Partitioning is optional, just as for other window functions, and ORDER BY is required. Here is the basic syntax:

```
LAG (<column you need>) OVER([PARTITION BY <expression>] ORDER BY
<expression>)
LEAD (<column you need>) OVER([PARTITION BY <expression>] ORDER BY
<expression>)
```

Run Listing 6-1 to see LAG and LEAD in action.

© Kathi Kellenberger, Clayton Groom, and Ed Pollack 2019
K. Kellenberger et al., *Expert T-SQL Window Functions in SQL Server 2019*,
https://doi.org/10.1007/978-1-4842-5197-3_6

Listing 6-1. Using LAG and LEAD

```
--6-1.1 Use LAG and LEAD
SELECT CustomerID, SalesOrderID, CAST(OrderDate AS DATE) AS OrderDate,
    LAG(CAST(OrderDate AS DATE)) OVER(PARTITION BY CustomerID
        ORDER BY SalesOrderID) AS PrevOrderDate,
    LEAD(CAST(OrderDate AS DATE)) OVER(PARTITION BY CustomerID
        ORDER BY SalesOrderID) AS NextOrderDate
FROM Sales.SalesOrderHeader;

--6-1.2 Use LAG and LEAD as an argument
SELECT CustomerID, SalesOrderID, CAST(OrderDate AS DATE) AS OrderDate,
    DATEDIFF(DAY,LAG(OrderDate)
        OVER(PARTITION BY CustomerID ORDER BY SalesOrderID), OrderDate)
        AS DaysSincePrevOrder,
    DATEDIFF(DAY, OrderDate, LEAD(OrderDate)
        OVER(PARTITION BY CustomerID ORDER BY SalesOrderID))
        AS DaysUntilNextOrder
FROM Sales.SalesOrderHeader;
```

Figure 6-1 shows the partial results. Query 1 uses the LAG and LEAD functions to find the previous and next order dates relative to the current row. The argument for the functions is the OrderDate cast to the DATE data type. Just like the other window functions, PARTITION BY is optional. In this case, the data is partitioned by the CustomerID. The ORDER BY is a very important part of the OVER clause. It determines which row is the previous row and which row is the next row. Query 2 has the same OVER clauses as Query 1. The difference is that the LAG and LEAD expressions are used as arguments to the DATEDIFF functions to determine the number of days between orders.

	CustomerID	SalesOrderID	OrderDate	PrevOrderDate	NextOrderDate
1	11000	43793	2011-06-21	NULL	2013-06-20
2	11000	51522	2013-06-20	2011-06-21	2013-10-03
3	11000	57418	2013-10-03	2013-06-20	NULL
4	11001	43767	2011-06-17	NULL	2013-06-18
5	11001	51493	2013-06-18	2011-06-17	2014-05-12
6	11001	72773	2014-05-12	2013-06-18	NULL

	CustomerID	SalesOrderID	OrderDate	DaysSincePrevOrder	DaysUntilNextOrd...
1	11000	43793	2011-06-21	NULL	730
2	11000	51522	2013-06-20	730	105
3	11000	57418	2013-10-03	105	NULL
4	11001	43767	2011-06-17	NULL	732
5	11001	51493	2013-06-18	732	328
6	11001	72773	2014-05-12	328	NULL

Figure 6-1. *Partial results of the LAG and LEAD functions*

Note that there are several NULL values in the results. Row 1 is the first row of the partition. You cannot find an earlier row, so NULL is returned for PrevOrderDate and DaysSincePrevOrder. Row 3 is the final row of the partition. There is no row past row 3 in the partition so NextOrderDate and DaysUntilNextOrder are null for row 3.

So far, you have seen the default ways to use LAG and LEAD. These functions each have two optional parameters. The first parameter is the Offset, which is 1 by default. By default, LEAD pulls an expression from one row before the current row, and LAG pulls an expression from one row past the current row. By using the Offset parameter, you can access columns from rows farther away than one. One interesting thing to note about the offset is that only positive integers are allowed. When using LAG, a positive number means "go backward." When using LEAD, a positive number means "go forward." Here is the syntax for using the Offset parameter:

```
LAG(<column> [,<offset>]) OVER(<over clause expression>)
LEAD(<column> [,<offset>]) OVER(<over clause expression>)
```

Listing 6-2 demonstrates how to use the Offset parameter.

Listing 6-2. Using the Offset Parameter with LAG

```
--6-2.1 Using Offset with LAG
WITH Totals AS (
    SELECT YEAR(OrderDate) AS OrderYear,
        MONTH(OrderDate)/4 + 1 AS OrderQtr,
        SUM(TotalDue) AS TotalSales
        FROM Sales.SalesOrderHeader
    GROUP BY YEAR(OrderDate), MONTH(OrderDate)/4 + 1)
SELECT OrderYear, Totals.OrderQtr, TotalSales,
    LAG(TotalSales, 4) OVER(ORDER BY OrderYear, OrderQtr)
        AS PreviousYearsSales
FROM Totals
ORDER BY OrderYear, OrderQtr;
```

Figure 6-2 shows the results. In this example, the total is aggregated by the year and calendar quarter in a CTE. The calendar quarter is calculated by finding the month, dividing by four and adding one. In the outer query, by using LAG with an offset of four, the previous year's sales for the same quarter are returned. Note that this method will only work if there are no gaps in the data, since it is using a physical offset and not a logical one. To prove that the results are correct, compare the PreviousYearSales of row 8, the first quarter of 2013, to the TotalSales of row 4, the first quarter of 2012.

	OrderYear	OrderQtr	TotalSales	PreviousYearsSales
1	2011	2	3366300.3016	NULL
2	2011	3	9326950.3248	NULL
3	2011	4	1462448.8986	NULL
4	2012	1	9443736.8161	NULL
5	2012	2	13775726.6319	3366300.3016
6	2012	3	11279388.6953	9326950.3248
7	2012	4	3176848.1687	1462448.8986
8	2013	1	8771886.3577	9443736.8161
9	2013	2	17746902.2275	13775726.6319
10	2013	3	17886522.2822	11279388.6953
11	2013	4	4560577.0958	3176848.1687
12	2014	1	14373277.4766	8771886.3577
13	2014	2	8046220.8391	17746902.2275

Figure 6-2. *The results of using the Offset with LAG*

The first four rows of the results return NULL for the PreviousYearSales. That is because there is no row with an offset of four from the current row until you get to row 5. If returning NULLs is a problem, you can use the second optional parameter to replace NULLs with a default value. In order to use the second parameter, you must also fill in the first parameter. Here is the syntax:

```
LAG(<column> [,<offset>] [,<default>]) OVER(<over clause expression>)
LEAD(<column> [,<offset>] [,<default>]) OVER(<over clause expression>)
```

Listing 6-3 demonstrates how to use the Default parameter.

Listing 6-3. Using the Default Parameter with LAG

```
--6-3.1 Using Offset with LAG
WITH Totals AS (
    SELECT YEAR(OrderDate) AS OrderYear,
        MONTH(OrderDate)/4 + 1 AS OrderQtr,
        SUM(TotalDue) AS TotalSales
        FROM Sales.SalesOrderHeader
    GROUP BY YEAR(OrderDate), MONTH(OrderDate)/4 + 1)
```

```
SELECT OrderYear, Totals.OrderQtr, TotalSales,
    LAG(TotalSales, 4, 0) OVER(ORDER BY OrderYear, OrderQtr)
        AS PreviousYearsSales
FROM Totals
ORDER BY OrderYear, OrderQtr;
```

Figure 6-3 shows the results. This query is the same as the query from Listing 6-2 with the addition of the Default parameter. All NULL values in PreviousYearSales have been changed to zero. Of course, you can use both the Offset and Default with LEAD as well.

	OrderYear	OrderQtr	TotalSales	PreviousYearsSales
1	2011	2	3366300.3016	0.00
2	2011	3	9326950.3248	0.00
3	2011	4	1462448.8986	0.00
4	2012	1	9443736.8161	0.00
5	2012	2	13775726.6319	3366300.3016
6	2012	3	11279388.6953	9326950.3248
7	2012	4	3176848.1687	1462448.8986
8	2013	1	8771886.3577	9443736.8161
9	2013	2	17746902.2275	13775726.6319
10	2013	3	17886522.2822	11279388.6953
11	2013	4	4560577.0958	3176848.1687
12	2014	1	14373277.4766	8771886.3577
13	2014	2	8046220.8391	17746902.2275

Figure 6-3. *The results using the Default parameter with LAG*

Understanding FIRST_VALUE and LAST_VALUE

While LAG and LEAD allow you to include any column from a row a given number of rows away from the current row, the FIRST_VALUE and LAST_VALUE functions let you include any column from the first or last row of the partition. At first glance, this may seem very similar to MIN and MAX, but they are very different. The column to sort on is not necessarily the column to pull into the results. The first value may not be the minimum value. These functions do not have any optional parameters, but they do support framing. Review Chapter 5 to learn more about framing if you are not familiar with the concept. Recall that the default frame starts at the first row of the partition and includes all rows up to the current row. This causes a problem when using LAST_VALUE. If you do not specify the frame, LAST_VALUE returns the value from the current row instead of from the last row of the partition. That is because the current row is the same as the last row with the default frame. Listing 6-4 demonstrates how to use FIRST_VALUE and LAST_VALUE.

Listing 6-4. Using FIRST_VALUE and LAST_VALUE

```
--6-4.1 Using FIRST_VALUE and LAST_VALUE
SELECT CustomerID, SalesOrderID, TotalDue,
    FIRST_VALUE(TotalDue) OVER(PARTITION BY CustomerID
        ORDER BY SalesOrderID) AS FirstOrderAmt,
    LAST_VALUE(TotalDue) OVER(PARTITION BY CustomerID
        ORDER BY SalesOrderID) AS LastOrderAmt_WRONG,
    LAST_VALUE(TotalDue) OVER(PARTITION BY CustomerID
        ORDER BY SalesOrderID
        ROWS BETWEEN CURRENT ROW AND UNBOUNDED FOLLOWING) AS LastOrderAmt
FROM Sales.SalesOrderHeader
ORDER BY CustomerID, SalesOrderID;
```

Figure 6-4 shows the partial results. The windows are partitioned by CustomerID and ordered by SalesOrderID. The query itself is ordered by CustomerID and SalesOrderID so you can verify the results. Take a look at row 2. The FirstOrderAmt correctly returns the value of the TotalDue from row 1. The window frame for FirstOrderAmt is the default, all rows from the beginning of the partition up to the current row. Since the frame was not specified for LastOrderAmt_WRONG, the frame is the same, which only goes up to the current row. The query was intended to pull a value from the very last row of the partition, however. In order to do that, the frame must be specified. The expression for LastOrderAmt includes the correct frame so it actually does return the expected value.

	CustomerID	SalesOrderID	TotalDue	FirstOrderAmt	LastOrderAmt_WRONG	LastOrderAmt
1	11000	43793	3756.989	3756.989	3756.989	2770.2682
2	11000	51522	2587.8769	3756.989	2587.8769	2770.2682
3	11000	57418	2770.2682	3756.989	2770.2682	2770.2682
4	11001	43767	3729.364	3729.364	3729.364	650.8008
5	11001	51493	2674.0227	3729.364	2674.0227	650.8008
6	11001	72773	650.8008	3729.364	650.8008	650.8008
7	11002	43736	3756.989	3756.989	3756.989	2673.0613
8	11002	51238	2535.964	3756.989	2535.964	2673.0613

Figure 6-4. *Partial results of using FIRST_VALUE and LAST_VALUE*

The new graph database function SHORTEST_PATH uses it without an OVER clause. Take a look at this article to learn more: `https://www.red-gate.com/simple-talk/sql/sql-development/sql-server-2019-graph-database-and-shortest_path/`.

Using the Offset Functions to Solve Queries

My favorite T-SQL functions of all time are LAG and LEAD. Not only are they easy to use, but they perform very well, too. You will learn more about how the performance of the offset functions compares to other methods in Chapter 8. In Chapter 1, you saw how easy it was to compare closing stock prices using LAG. Now you will see how offset functions can be used to solve some other real-world problems.

The Year-Over-Year Growth Calculation

Year-over-year (YOY) growth is a very commonly used metric in business. It compares a period, such as a month or quarter, to the same period from the previous year. Run Listing 6-5 to see how easy this is to do with LAG.

Listing 6-5. Calculating YOY Growth with LAG

```
--6-5.1 Calculate Year-Over-Year Growth
WITH
Level1 AS (
    SELECT YEAR(OrderDate) AS SalesYear,
        MONTH(OrderDate) AS SalesMonth,
        SUM(TotalDue) AS TotalSales
```

```
FROM Sales.SalesOrderHeader
GROUP BY YEAR(OrderDate), MONTH(OrderDate)
),
Level2 AS (
    SELECT SalesYear, SalesMonth,TotalSales,
        LAG(TotalSales,12) OVER(ORDER BY SalesYear) AS PrevYearSales
    FROM Level1)
SELECT SalesYear, SalesMonth,FORMAT(TotalSales,'C') AS TotalSales,
    FORMAT(PrevYearSales,'C') AS PrevYearSales,
    FORMAT((TotalSales-PrevYearSales)/PrevYearSales,'P') AS YOY_Growth
FROM Level2
WHERE PrevYearSales IS NOT NULL;
```

Figure 6-5 shows the partial results. In order to demonstrate a stepwise approach, this query contains two CTEs. Except for filtering out the NULL values, the same results could be obtained by writing the query at two levels, but I think this approach makes it easier to understand. The first CTE, Level1, creates a list of sales by year and month. Level2 adds in the expression using LAG to calculate the sales for the same month of the previous year. Finally, in the outer query, the YOY calculation is performed by subtracting the previous year's sales from the current sales and dividing by the previous year's sales. The FORMAT function is used to change the results to a percentage. The rows that cannot be compared to a previous row are filtered out of the outer query.

	SalesYear	SalesMonth	TotalSales	PrevYearSales	YOY_Growth
1	2012	3	$3,336,347.47	$1,462,448.90	128.13 %
2	2012	9	$3,881,724.19	$507,096.47	665.48 %
3	2012	8	$2,442,451.18	$554,791.61	340.24 %
4	2012	2	$1,649,051.90	$5,156,269.53	-68.01 %
5	2012	11	$2,097,153.13	$2,292,182.88	-8.50 %
6	2012	7	$3,840,231.46	$567,020.95	577.26 %
7	2012	5	$3,452,924.45	$2,800,576.17	23.29 %
8	2012	10	$2,858,060.20	$815,313.02	250.54 %

Figure 6-5. Partial results of calculating YOY growth

The Timecard Problem

This problem involves the timecards of employees as they arrive at and leave work each day. The goal is to calculate how long each employee worked on each shift. Listing 6-6 contains the statements to create a temp table and display the initial rows.

Listing 6-6. Create and Populate the #TimeCard Table

```
--6-6.1 Create the table
DROP TABLE IF EXISTS #TimeCards;
CREATE TABLE #TimeCards(
    TimeStampID INT NOT NULL IDENTITY PRIMARY KEY,
    EmployeeID INT NOT NULL,
    ClockDateTime DATETIME2(0) NOT NULL,
    EventType VARCHAR(5) NOT NULL);

--6-6.2 Populate the table
INSERT INTO #TimeCards(EmployeeID,
    ClockDateTime, EventType)
VALUES
    (1,'2019-01-02 08:00','ENTER'),
    (2,'2019-01-02 08:03','ENTER'),
    (2,'2019-01-02 12:00','EXIT'),
    (2,'2019-01-02 12:34','Enter'),
    (3,'2019-01-02 16:30','ENTER'),
    (2,'2019-01-02 16:00','EXIT'),
    (1,'2019-01-02 16:07','EXIT'),
    (3,'2019-01-03 01:00','EXIT'),
    (2,'2019-01-03 08:10','ENTER'),
    (1,'2019-01-03 08:15','ENTER'),
    (2,'2019-01-03 12:17','EXIT'),
    (3,'2019-01-03 16:00','ENTER'),
    (1,'2019-01-03 15:59','EXIT'),
    (3,'2019-01-04 01:00','EXIT');

--6-6.2 Display the rows
SELECT TimeStampID, EmployeeID, ClockDateTime, EventType
FROM #TimeCards;
```

Figure 6-6 shows the rows for this problem. Note that every ENTER row has a matching EXIT row.

	TimeStampID	EmployeeID	ClockDateTime	EventType
1	1	1	2019-01-02 08:00:00	ENTER
2	2	2	2019-01-02 08:03:00	ENTER
3	3	2	2019-01-02 12:00:00	EXIT
4	4	2	2019-01-02 12:34:00	Enter
5	5	3	2019-01-02 16:30:00	ENTER
6	6	2	2019-01-02 16:00:00	EXIT
7	7	1	2019-01-02 16:07:00	EXIT
8	8	3	2019-01-03 01:00:00	EXIT
9	9	2	2019-01-03 08:10:00	ENTER
10	10	1	2019-01-03 08:15:00	ENTER
11	11	2	2019-01-03 12:17:00	EXIT
12	12	3	2019-01-03 16:00:00	ENTER
13	13	1	2019-01-03 15:59:00	EXIT
14	14	3	2019-01-04 01:00:00	EXIT

Figure 6-6. The timecard rows

Solving this problem is easy with the LEAD function. Listing 6-7 shows the solution.

Listing 6-7. The Solution to the Timecard Problem

```
WITH Level1 AS (
    SELECT EmployeeID, EventType, ClockDateTime,
        LEAD(ClockDateTime) OVER(PARTITION BY EmployeeID ORDER BY
        ClockDateTime)
            AS NextDateTime
    FROM #TimeCards
),
Level2 AS (
    SELECT EmployeeID, CAST(ClockDateTime AS DATE) AS WorkDate,
        SUM(DATEDIFF(second, ClockDateTime,NextDateTime)) AS Seconds
```

```
    FROM Level1
    WHERE EventType = 'Enter'
    GROUP BY EmployeeID, CAST(ClockDateTime AS DATE))
SELECT EmployeeID, WorkDate,
    TIMEFROMPARTS(Seconds / 3600, Seconds % 3600 / 60,
        Seconds % 3600 % 60, 0, 0) AS HoursWorked
FROM Level2
ORDER BY EmployeeID, WorkDate;
```

The solution is split up to make it easier to understand. The first CTE, Level1, uses the LEAD function to find the ClockDateTime of the next row. The number of seconds between the two is calculated and the Exit rows are thrown out. The seconds are also summed in this level in case the employee clocked out for lunch. The main query uses the TIMEFROMPARTS to convert the seconds into an hour:minute format. Figure 6-7 shows the results.

	EmployeeID	WorkDate	HoursWorked
1	1	2019-01-02	08:07:00
2	1	2019-01-03	07:44:00
3	2	2019-01-02	07:23:00
4	2	2019-01-03	04:07:00
5	3	2019-01-02	08:30:00
6	3	2019-01-03	09:00:00

Figure 6-7. *The results of the timecard problem*

Summary

The offset functions of LAG, LEAD, FIRST_VALUE, and LAST_VALUE first available with SQL Server 2012 are very powerful. They not only make it easy to write queries that pull values from different rows, but the performance is fantastic, too, which you'll see for yourself in Chapter 8.

There is one more set of functions to learn, the statistical functions. Chapter 7 teaches you what you need to know to take advantage of these window functions.

CHAPTER 7

Understanding Statistical Functions

In 2012, Microsoft added four more window functions to SQL Server. These are statistical functions PERCENT_RANK, CUME_DIST, PERCENTILE_CONT, and PERCENTILE_DISC. These functions make analyzing data from many sources, such as science, academics, or sports, easy.

In this chapter you will learn how to use these statistical functions.

Using PERCENT_RANK and CUME_DIST

Remember those standardized tests you took in school? You were probably given a raw score and a percent for each area tested, such as mathematics or language skills. Percent rank is a way to calculate how each individual in a group compares to the rest of the group.

Starting with SQL Server 2012, there are two functions for ranking data such as those test scores, or even heights. Say that there are 100 seventh graders lined up by height. My grandson, Thomas, is a pretty tall boy so he would stand at spot 95. He is taller than 94 other students. His height is higher than 94% of the heights and is higher than or the same as 95% of the heights. Thomas' height has a PERCENT_RANK of 0.9494 and a CUME_DIST (cumulative distribution) of 0.95.

You may be wondering why the PERCENT_RANK is 0.9494 and not just 0.94. The formula for PERCENT_RANK is the rank of the score minus one divided by the number of scores minus one: (rank-1)/(N-1). The formula for CUME_DIST is just the rank of the score divided by the number of scores: rank/N. The PERCENT_RANK of Thomas' height can be found by dividing 94 by 99, not 94 by 100.

© Kathi Kellenberger, Clayton Groom, and Ed Pollack 2019
K. Kellenberger et al., *Expert T-SQL Window Functions in SQL Server 2019*,
https://doi.org/10.1007/978-1-4842-5197-3_7

Just like all other window functions, an OVER clause is required when using these functions. It must contain an ORDER BY expression that determines how the scores or values are lined up. The PARTITION BY expression is optional. If it is used, then the items within a partition will be compared, not outside the partition. Here is the syntax:

```
PERCENT_RANK OVER([PARTITION BY <expression>] ORDER BY <expression>)
CUME_DIST OVER([PARTITION BY <expression>] ORDER BY <expression>)
```

Listing 7-1 demonstrates how to use these functions to compare the sales for each month of a given year.

Listing 7-1. Using PERCENT_RANK and CUME_DIST

```
--7-1.1 Using PERCENT_RANK and CUME_DIST
SELECT COUNT(*) NumberOfOrders, Month(OrderDate) AS OrderMonth,
    RANK() OVER(ORDER BY COUNT(*)) AS Ranking,
    PERCENT_RANK() OVER(ORDER BY COUNT(*)) AS PercentRank,
    CUME_DIST() OVER(ORDER BY COUNT(*)) AS CumeDist
FROM Sales.SalesOrderHeader
WHERE OrderDate >= '2013-01-01' AND OrderDate < '2014-01-01'
GROUP BY  Month(OrderDate);
```

Figure 7-1 shows the results. The query is filtered to include the orders for just 2013 and grouped by month. The ORDER BY expression for each function is the count of the orders. Recall that when you use a window function in an aggregate query, any columns used in the function must follow the rules for the SELECT list. See Chapter 3 for more information about adding a window function to an aggregate query. The PercentRank for the first row is 0. The first value for PercentRank will always be 0 because that row is not ranked above any other row. Both the PercentRank and CumeDist will be 1, or 100% for the last row. In all rows except for the last, the CumeDist is larger than the PercentRank. Notice that when there is a tie, as in rows 3 and 4, the values are repeated.

	NumberOfOrders	OrderMonth	Ranking	PercentRank	CumeDist
1	325	2	1	0	0.0833333333333333
2	400	1	2	0.0909090909090909	0.166666666666667
3	428	4	3	0.181818181818182	0.333333333333333
4	428	5	3	0.181818181818182	0.333333333333333
5	441	3	5	0.363636363636364	0.416666666666667
6	719	6	6	0.454545454545455	0.5
7	1740	7	7	0.545454545454545	0.583333333333333
8	1789	8	8	0.636363636363636	0.666666666666667
9	1791	9	9	0.727272727272727	0.75
10	1968	10	10	0.818181818181818	0.833333333333333
11	2050	12	11	0.909090909090909	0.916666666666667
12	2103	11	12	1	1

Figure 7-1. *The results of using PERCENT_RANK and CUME_DIST*

Here's another example comparing the average high monthly temperature for the St. Louis Metro area where I live. Run Listing 7-2 to create and populate the table.

Listing 7-2. The St. Louis Average High Temps

```
--7-2.1 Create the table
CREATE TABLE #MonthlyTempsStl(MNo Int, MName varchar(15), AvgHighTempF INT,
AvgHighTempC DECIMAL(4,2));

--7-2.2 Insert the rows with F temps
INSERT INTO #MonthlyTempsStl (Mno, Mname, AvgHighTempF)
VALUES(1,'Jan',40),(2,'Feb',45),(3,'Mar',55),(4,'Apr',67),(5,'May',77),
(6,'Jun',85),
        (7,'Jul',89),(8,'Aug',88),(9,'Sep',81),(10,'Oct',69),(11,'Nov',56),
        (12,'Dec',43);

--7-2.3 Calculate C
UPDATE #MonthlyTempsStl
SET AvgHighTempC = (AvgHighTempF - 32) * 5.0/9;

--7-2.4 Return the results
SELECT * FROM #MonthlyTempsStl;
```

Figure 7-2 shows the rows in the table.

	MNo	MName	AvgHighTempF	AvgHighTempC
1	1	Jan	40	4.44
2	2	Feb	45	7.22
3	3	Mar	55	12.78
4	4	Apr	67	19.44
5	5	May	77	25.00
6	6	Jun	85	29.44
7	7	Jul	89	31.67
8	8	Aug	88	31.11
9	9	Sep	81	27.22
10	10	Oct	69	20.56
11	11	Nov	56	13.33
12	12	Dec	43	6.11

Figure 7-2. *The average monthly high temperatures*

Listing 7-3 returns the percent rank and cumulative distribution of the temperatures.

Listing 7-3. Ranking the Temperatures

```
--7-3.1 Ranking the temps
SELECT MName, AvgHighTempF, AvgHighTempC,
       PERCENT_RANK() OVER(ORDER BY AvgHighTempF) * 100.0 AS PR,
       CUME_DIST() OVER(ORDER BY AvgHighTempF) * 100.0 AS CD
FROM #MonthlyTempsStl;
```

Figure 7-3 shows the results. January is the coldest month, while July is the hottest. Just like the first example, both the percent rank and cumulative distribution are at 100 in July.

	MName	AvgHighTempF	AvgHighTempC	PR	CD
1	Jan	40	4.44	0	8.33333333333333
2	Dec	43	6.11	9.09090909090909	16.6666666666667
3	Feb	45	7.22	18.1818181818182	25
4	Mar	55	12.78	27.2727272727273	33.3333333333333
5	Nov	56	13.33	36.3636363636364	41.6666666666667
6	Apr	67	19.44	45.4545454545455	50
7	Oct	69	20.56	54.5454545454545	58.3333333333333
8	May	77	25.00	63.6363636363636	66.6666666666667
9	Sep	81	27.22	72.7272727272727	75
10	Jun	85	29.44	81.8181818181818	83.3333333333333
11	Aug	88	31.11	90.9090909090909	91.6666666666667
12	Jul	89	31.67	100	100

Figure 7-3. *The temperatures ranked*

Using PERCENTILE_CONT and PERCENTILE_DISC

You have seen how to rank and compare a series of values with PERCENT_RANK and CUME_DIST. The other two statistical functions, PERCENTILE_CONT (percentile continuous) and PERCENTILE_DISC (percentile discrete), perform the opposite task. Given a percent rank, these functions find the value at that position. The difference between these two functions is that PERCENTILE_CONT interpolates a value over the set while PERCENTILE_DISC returns an exact value from the set.

One very common requirement is to find the median, or middle value in a list of values. You can accomplish this task by using PERCENTILE_CONT and specifying that you wish to find the value at 50%.

The syntax of these functions is also a bit different compared to the other window functions. You still need to supply an OVER clause, but inside the OVER clause you only specify the PARTITION BY expression if one is needed.

Instead of placing the ORDER BY in the OVER clause, there is a new clause called WITHIN GROUP, where the ORDER BY will go. The WITHIN GROUP clause must return a list of numbers. Recall that the ORDER BY in the OVER clause for other functions lines up the rows, but in this case, the WITHIN GROUP expression is the list of numbers to operate on. The ORDER BY must contain just one expression and evaluate to a numeric type like INT or DECIMAL.

Here is the syntax:

```
PERCENTILE_CONT(<percent to find>) WITHIN GROUP(ORDER BY <expression>)
    OVER([PARTITION BY <expression>])
PERCENTILE_DISC(<percent to find>) WITHIN GROUP(ORDER BY <expression>)
    OVER([PARTITION BY <expression>])
```

For the results shown in Figure 7-1 in the previous section, what is the median? Since an even number of rows is returned, it is the average of 719 and 1740, or 1229.5. Listing 7-4 demonstrates how the median can be calculated with PERCENTILE_ CONT. PERCENTILE_DISC is shown as well, but it is not the median because there is an even number of rows. The answer is returned on every row; if you wish to see just the answer, use DISTINCT.

Listing 7-4. Finding the Median with PERCENTILE_CONT

```
--7-4.1 Find median for the set
SELECT COUNT(*) NumberOfOrders, Month(OrderDate) AS orderMonth,
    PERCENTILE_CONT(.5) WITHIN GROUP (ORDER BY COUNT(*))
    OVER() AS TheMedian,
    PERCENTILE_DISC(.5) WITHIN GROUP (ORDER BY COUNT(*))
    OVER() AS PercentileDisc
FROM Sales.SalesOrderHeader
WHERE OrderDate >= '2013-01-01' AND OrderDate < '2014-01-01'
GROUP BY Month(OrderDate);

--7-4.2 Return just the answer
SELECT  DISTINCT PERCENTILE_CONT(.5) WITHIN GROUP (ORDER BY COUNT(*))
    OVER() AS TheMedian,
    PERCENTILE_DISC(.5) WITHIN GROUP (ORDER BY COUNT(*))
    OVER() AS PercentileDisc
FROM Sales.SalesOrderHeader
WHERE OrderDate >= '2013-01-01' AND OrderDate < '2014-01-01'
GROUP BY Month(OrderDate);
```

The results are shown in Figure 7-4. Query 1 shows the count and month for the entire year along with the TheMedian and PercentileDisc. The values are the same for every row because the answer is the same for every row in the set. Query 2 removes the count and month and uses DISTINCT so that just the answers are returned. Notice that

Percentile_Cont interpolates the answer by averaging the two middle values producing a true median. Percentile_Disc, however, returns a value of 719. This is an actual value in the set. If the number of values is even, then this function will return the first value closest to the median when the percentile to compute is 0.5.

	NumberOfOrders	orderMonth	TheMedian	PercentileDisc
1	325	2	1229.5	719
2	400	1	1229.5	719
3	428	4	1229.5	719
4	428	5	1229.5	719
5	441	3	1229.5	719
6	719	6	1229.5	719
7	1740	7	1229.5	719
8	1789	8	1229.5	719
9	1791	9	1229.5	719
10	1968	10	1229.5	719
11	2050	12	1229.5	719
12	2103	11	1229.5	719

	TheMedian	PercentileDisc
1	1229.5	719

Figure 7-4. Finding the median

When there is an odd number of rows, these functions will return the same value in this case. Listing 7-5 shows what happens if there is an odd number of rows by filtering out one month.

Listing 7-5. Finding the Median with an Odd Number of Rows

```
--7-5.1 Filter out January
SELECT  DISTINCT PERCENTILE_CONT(.5) WITHIN GROUP (ORDER BY COUNT(*))
    OVER() AS TheMedian,
    PERCENTILE_DISC(.5) WITHIN GROUP (ORDER BY COUNT(*))
    OVER() AS PercentileDisc
FROM Sales.SalesOrderHeader
WHERE OrderDate >= '2013-02-01' AND OrderDate < '2014-01-01'
GROUP BY Month(OrderDate);
```

Figure 7-5 shows the results. In this case, since the number of rows is odd, the two functions return the same value.

	TheMedian	PercentileDisc
1	1740	1740

Figure 7-5. *The two functions return the same value with odd rows*

While finding the median is an interesting use for these functions, you can also use them to find the value at any other percent rank. A useful application of this would be to return the value at the top 25% position, for example. Listing 7-6 creates and populates a temp table with student scores and returns the score found at the top 25% position.

Listing 7-6. Finding the Score at the Top 25% Position

```
--7-6.1 Set up table
CREATE TABLE #scores(StudentID INT IDENTITY, Score DECIMAL(5,2));

--7-6.2
--Insert scores with Itzik style numbers table
WITH lv0 AS (SELECT 0 g UNION ALL SELECT 0)
    ,lv1 AS (SELECT 0 g FROM lv0 a CROSS JOIN lv0 b)
    ,lv2 AS (SELECT 0 g FROM lv1 a CROSS JOIN lv1 b)
    ,lv3 AS (SELECT 0 g FROM lv2 a CROSS JOIN lv2 b)
    ,lv4 AS (SELECT 0 g FROM lv3 a CROSS JOIN lv3 b)
    ,Tally (n) AS (SELECT ROW_NUMBER() OVER (ORDER BY (SELECT NULL))
                FROM lv4)
INSERT INTO #scores(Score)
SELECT TOP(1000) CAST(RAND(CHECKSUM(NEWID())) * 100 as DECIMAL(5,2)) AS
Score
FROM Tally;

--7-6.3 Return the score at the top 25%
SELECT DISTINCT PERCENTILE_DISC(.25) WITHIN GROUP
    (ORDER BY Score DESC) OVER() AS Top25
FROM #scores;
```

Figure 7-6 shows the result. Your value will be different, of course, since the scores were generated randomly. After setting up the variables and the table, 1,000 rows were inserted with a random value. Query 3 returns the score at the top 25% position by finding the score with PERCENTILE_DISC 0.25 and sorting the scores in descending order.

	Top25
1	74.97

Figure 7-6. *The score at the top 25% position*

Comparing Statistical Functions to Older Methods

The functions PERCENT_RANK and CUME_DIST are more of a convenience than an amazing breakthrough like the offset functions you learned about in Chapter 6. By using the RANK function in a simple calculation, you can come up with the same answers. The formulas are as follows:

```
PERCENT_RANK = (Rank - 1)/(N - 1)
CUME_DIST = Rank/N
```

Listing 7-7 demonstrates that you can get the same results as Listing 7-1 by using SQL Server 2005 functionality.

Listing 7-7. Using SQL Server 2005 Functionality for the Same Results

```
--7-7.1 Using 2005 functionality
SELECT COUNT(*) NumberOfOrders, Month(OrderDate) AS OrderMonth,
    ((RANK() OVER(ORDER BY COUNT(*)) -1) * 1.0)/(COUNT(*) OVER() -1)
    AS PercentRank,
    (RANK() OVER(ORDER BY COUNT(*)) * 1.0)/COUNT(*) OVER()
    AS CumeDist
FROM Sales.SalesOrderHeader
WHERE OrderDate >= '2013-01-01' AND OrderDate < '2014-01-01'
GROUP BY  Month(OrderDate);
```

Figure 7-7 shows the results. Except that the zeros are filled out to 12 places, the results look the same. In this example, the window aggregate, COUNT(*) OVER, is used to calculate the number of rows in the partition. For PercentRank, one is subtracted from both the rank and the count before dividing.

	NumberOfOrders	OrderMonth	PercentRank	CumeDist
1	325	2	0.000000000000	0.083333333333
2	400	1	0.090909090909	0.166666666666
3	428	4	0.181818181818	0.250000000000
4	428	5	0.181818181818	0.250000000000
5	441	3	0.363636363636	0.416666666666
6	719	6	0.454545454545	0.500000000000
7	1740	7	0.545454545454	0.583333333333
8	1789	8	0.636363636363	0.666666666666
9	1791	9	0.727272727272	0.750000000000
10	1968	10	0.818181818181	0.833333333333
11	2050	12	0.909090909090	0.916666666666
12	2103	11	1.000000000000	1.000000000000

Figure 7-7. *The results of calculating percents with older methods*

Is it possible to use an older method for the PERCENTILE_CONT and PERCENTILE_DISC functions? It is not difficult for PERCENTILE_DISC because it always returns an actual value from the set. Listing 7-8 shows how to calculate PERCENTILE_DISC using only 2005 functionality.

Listing 7-8. Using Only SQL Server 2005 Functionality to Calculate PERCENTILE_DISC

```
--7-8.1 PERCENTILE_DISC
SELECT DISTINCT PERCENTILE_DISC(0.75) WITHIN GROUP (ORDER BY COUNT(*))
OVER() AS PercentileDisc
FROM Sales.SalesOrderHeader
WHERE OrderDate >= '2013-01-01' AND OrderDate < '2014-01-01'
GROUP BY  Month(OrderDate);

--7-8.2 Old method
WITH Level1 AS (
    SELECT COUNT(*) NumberOfOrders,
        ((RANK() OVER(ORDER BY COUNT(*)) -1) * 1.0)/(COUNT(*) OVER() -1)
        AS PercentRank
```

```
    FROM Sales.SalesOrderHeader
    WHERE OrderDate >= '2013-01-01' AND OrderDate < '2014-01-01'
    GROUP BY  Month(OrderDate))
SELECT TOP(1) NumberOfOrders AS PercentileDisc
FROM Level1
WHERE Level1.PercentRank <= 0.75
ORDER BY Level1.PercentRank DESC;
```

Figure 7-8 shows the results. Query 1 uses the new functionality so that you can compare it to the older method. Query 2 moves the query to calculate the percent rank to a CTE called Level1. In the outer query, one row that is equal to or less than the percent rank 0.75 is returned.

	PercentileDisc
1	1791

	PercentileDisc
1	1791

Figure 7-8. *The result of using an older method for PERCENTILE_DISC*

Accomplishing the same thing for PERCENTILE_CONT is even trickier but can still be done. In this case, when the exact row is not available, a value is calculated by using one value above and one value below the given percent rank. When trying to find the median, you just average the two rows, but not when trying to find any other percent rank. Listing 7-9 shows the solution.

Listing 7-9. Finding PERCENTILE_CONT Using SQL Server 2005 Functionality

```
--7-9.1 PERCENTILE_CONT
SELECT DISTINCT PERCENTILE_CONT(0.75) WITHIN GROUP (ORDER BY COUNT(*))
OVER() AS PercentCont
FROM Sales.SalesOrderHeader
WHERE OrderDate >= '2013-01-01' AND OrderDate < '2014-01-01'
GROUP BY  Month(OrderDate);
```

```
WITH Level1 AS (
        SELECT ROW_NUMBER() OVER(ORDER BY COUNT(*)) AS RowNum,
                COUNT(*) AS NumberOfOrders,
                (COUNT(*) OVER() -1) * .75 + 1 AS TheRow
        FROM Sales.SalesOrderHeader
        WHERE OrderDate >= '2013-01-01' AND OrderDate < '2014-01-01'
        GROUP BY Month(OrderDate)),
Level2 AS (
        SELECT RowNum, NumberOfOrders,
                FLOOR(TheRow) AS TheBottomRow,
                CEILING(TheRow) AS TheTopRow,
                TheRow
        FROM Level1 ),
Level3 AS (
        SELECT SUM(CASE WHEN RowNum = TheBottomRow THEN NumberOfOrders END)
        AS BottomValue,
                SUM(CASE WHEN RowNum = TheTopRow THEN NumberOfOrders END) AS
                TopValue,
                MAX(TheRow % Level2.TheBottomRow) AS Diff
        FROM Level2)
SELECT Level3.BottomValue +
        (Level3.TopValue - Level3.BottomValue) * Diff
FROM Level3;
```

Figure 7-9 shows the results. Query 1 uses the PERCENTILE_CONT function so that you can compare to the older method. The Level1 CTE contains a query that lists the row numbers and the count of orders for each month. It also figures out which row has the correct value, TheRow, if an exact value was in the list. In this case, the row is 9.25. In Level2, the FLOOR function is used to find the row below TheRow (9), and the CEILING function is used to find the row above TheRow (10). In Level3, the values for the two rows are found along with a multiplier, MP. MP is the decimal part of TheRow (0.25). The code finds it by performing a modulus operation (9.25 % 9). The outer query adds the difference between the two rows multiplied by MP to the value of the bottom row. Whew!

	PercentCont
1	1835.25

	PercentCont
1	1835.25

Figure 7-9. *Comparing PERCENTILE_CONT to an older method*

Summary

Now that you have seen statistical functions PERCENT_RANK, CUME_DIST, PERCENTILE_
DISC, and PERCENTILE_CONT, you have used all of the window functions available
with SQL Server 2012 up to 2019. In Chapter 8, you will learn about the performance
considerations when using all the window functions.

Tuning for Better Performance

Microsoft has always promoted window functions as having better performance than older techniques. In many situations, this is true, but, in my opinion, the biggest advantage is that these functions have made solving tricky queries easier. In some cases, these functions replace cursors, temp tables, and triangular joins. They are quite powerful tools before performance is even considered.

There are, however, some things you need to know to make sure your queries run as fast as possible when you use window functions. Microsoft hasn't added any new functionality since 2012, but it has made some changes to query processing in recent versions that directly affect window function performance.

In this chapter, you will learn what to look for in execution plans, where the bottlenecks are, and how to create an index to help any query with a window function. You'll also learn how window functions compare to using older methods and when using an older method might be a good idea.

Using Execution Plans

Graphical execution plans make tuning T-SQL queries easier. You can compare the performance of multiple queries and look for bottlenecks within a query. If graphical execution plans are new to you, you may want to read *SQL Server 2017 Query Performance Tuning* by Grant Fritchey (Apress, 2018) or just follow along and see what you can learn.

For many years, database professionals have been using SQL Server Management Studio (SSMS) to run queries. Microsoft has not only updated the icons used in graphical execution plans since the first edition of this book, it has recently introduced a new

113

© Kathi Kellenberger, Clayton Groom, and Ed Pollack 2019
K. Kellenberger et al., *Expert T-SQL Window Functions in SQL Server 2019*,
https://doi.org/10.1007/978-1-4842-5197-3_8

cross-platform tool called Azure Data Studio (ADS) with execution plans that have a different look to them. To see the difference, run the simple query found in Listing 8-1 both in SSMS and ADS. Before running the query in SSMS, be sure to turn on the execution plan by typing CTRL + M. In ADS, just click Explain after running the query.

Listing 8-1. A Simple Query to Run

```
--8-1.1 A simple query
SELECT *
FROM HumanResources.Employee;
```

Figure 8-1 shows the two execution plans.

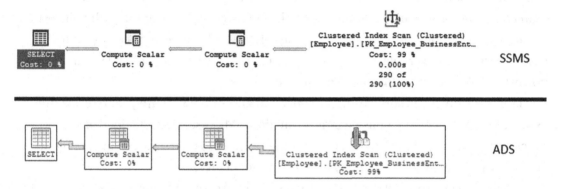

Figure 8-1. *The graphical execution plans from SSMS and ADS*

I'll show the execution plans generated from SSMS version 18 throughout this chapter. To follow along, be sure that the actual execution plan is toggled on for all examples in this chapter.

There is one execution operator that is specific for window functions; it is the *Sequence Project (Compute Scalar)* operator, which is shown in Figure 8-2. This operator is nothing to worry about. It just means that the column for the computation has been added to the results. You'll see it in the execution plans of queries with some window functions, but not all. To see the plan, run Listing 8-2.

Listing 8-2. Seeing the Sequence Project Operator (Compute Scalar)

```
--8-2.1 Query to produce Sequence Project (Compute Scalar) operator
SELECT CustomerID, ROW_NUMBER() OVER(ORDER BY SalesOrderID) AS RowNumber
FROM Sales.SalesOrderHeader;
```

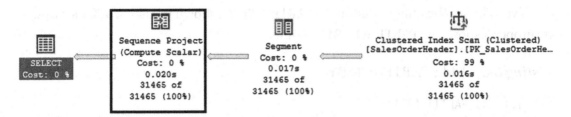

Figure 8-2. *An execution plan with a Sequence Project (Compute Scalar) operator*

Another operator you will see often with window function queries is the *Segment*
operator, also shown in Figure 8-2 to the right of the Sequence Project (Compute Scalar)
operator. The Segment operator divides the input into segments or groups. If there is no
PARTITION BY expression, then the segment will be the entire result set. Otherwise, the
segments will be divided by the PARTITION BY expressions. By opening the properties of
the Segment operator, you'll see that the Group By property is blank. Figure 8-3 shows this.

Properties	
Segment	
⊟ **Misc**	
Actual Execution Mode	Row
⊞ **Actual Number of Batches**	0
⊞ **Actual Number of Rows**	31465
⊞ **Actual Rebinds**	0
⊞ **Actual Rewinds**	0
⊞ **Actual Time Statistics**	
Description	Segment.
Estimated CPU Cost	0.0006293
Estimated Execution Mode	Row
Estimated I/O Cost	0
Estimated Number of Executions	1
Estimated Number of Rows	31465
Estimated Operator Cost	0.000629 (0%)
Estimated Rebinds	0
Estimated Rewinds	0
Estimated Row Size	19 B
Estimated Subtree Cost	0.545189
Group By	
Logical Operation	Segment
Node ID	1
Number of Executions	1
⊞ Output List	[AdventureWorks2017].[Sales].[Sales
Parallel	False
Physical Operation	Segment
⊞ Segment Column	Segment1003

Figure 8-3. *The Group By property of the Segment operator*

If you change the query by adding a PARTITION BY, shown in Listing 8-3, the Group By property shows the PARTITION BY column.

Listing 8-3. Add a PARTITION BY

```
--8-3.1 Add PARTITION BY
SELECT CustomerID,
  ROW_NUMBER() OVER(PARTITION BY CustomerID ORDER BY SalesOrderID) AS
  RowNumber
FROM Sales.SalesOrderHeader;
```

Figure 8-4 shows how the properties have changed.

Properties	
Segment	
⊟ **Misc**	
Actual Execution Mode	Row
⊞ Actual Number of Batches	0
⊞ Actual Number of Rows	31465
⊞ Actual Rebinds	0
⊞ Actual Rewinds	0
⊞ Actual Time Statistics	
Description	Segment.
Estimated CPU Cost	0.0006293
Estimated Execution Mode	Row
Estimated I/O Cost	0
Estimated Number of Executions	1
Estimated Number of Rows	31465
Estimated Operator Cost	0.0006293 (1%)
Estimated Rebinds	0
Estimated Rewinds	0
Estimated Row Size	19 B
Estimated Subtree Cost	0.0785228
⊟ Group By	[AdventureWorks2017].[Sales].[SalesOrderHeader].CustomerID
Column	CustomerID
Database	[AdventureWorks2017]
Schema	[Sales]
Table	[SalesOrderHeader]
Logical Operation	Segment
Node ID	1
Number of Executions	1
⊞ Output List	[AdventureWorks2017].[Sales].[SalesOrderHeader].SalesOrderID
Parallel	False
Physical Operation	Segment
⊞ Segment Column	Segment1003

Figure 8-4. *The Group By properties when a partition is added*

116

The Sequence Project (Compute Scalar) and Segment operators are nothing to worry about when tuning queries. The operator to watch out for, that you can do something about, is the *Sort* operator, shown in Figure 8-5. The Sort operator is found in many types of queries and is often the bottleneck in window function queries. To see the plan, run Listing 8-4.

Listing 8-4. A Query with a Sort Operator

```
--8-4.1 A query to show the Sort operator
SELECT CustomerID, SalesOrderID,
    ROW_NUMBER() OVER(PARTITION BY CustomerID ORDER BY OrderDate) AS
    RowNumber
FROM Sales.SalesOrderHeader;
```

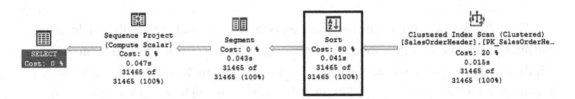

Figure 8-5. *An execution plan with the Sort operator*

Notice that the Sort operator takes 80% of the resources used to run the query even though a clustered index scan was performed. You'll learn how to create an index to eliminate the Sort in many cases later in the chapter.

There are two more operators to watch out for. Take a look at the Table Spool operator shown in Figure 8-6. Run Listing 8-5 to generate the plan yourself.

Listing 8-5. A Query Containing Table Spool Operators

```
--8-5.1 A query with a Table Spool operator
SELECT CustomerID, SalesOrderID, SUM(TotalDue)
    OVER(PARTITION BY CustomerID) AS SubTotal
FROM Sales.SalesOrderHeader;
```

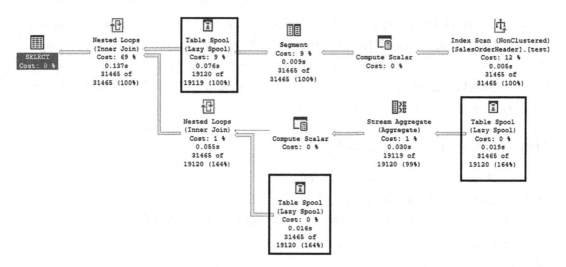

Figure 8-6. *An execution plan with Table Spool operators*

The Table Spool operator means that a worktable is created in `tempdb` to help solve the query. You will see Table Spool operators with window aggregates and some other window functions. This worktable uses a lot of resources, including locks, but there is good news if you are using SQL Server 2019 which you will learn about later in the chapter.

The other operator to be aware of, the Window Spool operator, is similar, but it *sometimes* creates the worktable in memory. Run Listing 8-6 to see the plan shown in Figure 8-7.

Listing 8-6. A Query Containing a Window Spool Operator

```
--8-6.1 A query isth a window spool operator
SELECT CustomerID, SalesOrderID, TotalDue,
    SUM(TotalDue) OVER(PARTITION BY CustomerID ORDER BY SalesOrderID) AS
    RunningTotal
FROM Sales.SalesOrderHeader;
```

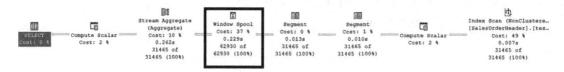

Figure 8-7. *A plan with a Window Spool operator*

The Window Spool operator theoretically means that the worktable is created in memory, but, in some cases, it is created in tempdb. The difference will be covered later in the chapter. Just like the Table Spool operator, this one has some performance improvements in 2019.

Using STATISTICS IO

Another very helpful tool for understanding query performance is STATISTICS IO. This setting will give you information about the pages read to run the query. The nice thing is that it doesn't matter if other queries are running on the server or if the data is already in the cache. If the cache is warm, meaning the needed data is already in memory, the query will often run faster, and you might mistakenly think you have made an improvement. The logical reads (the number of data pages read) returned will be consistent as long as nothing has changed about the query, indexes, data, or settings. That makes it a great tool for comparing two queries or figuring out if a new index has helped. I like to use both the execution plan and STATISTICS IO to make sure I understand what is going on.

Run Listing 8-7 to see how the queries from the previous section compare. While the queries do not produce the same results, it is still interesting to see the difference between them from a performance perspective. Note that the database compatibility mode has been set to the 2014 version.

Listing 8-7. Using STATISTICS IO

```
--8-7.0 Settings
USE [master];
GO
--Change database name as needed
ALTER DATABASE [AdventureWorks]
SET COMPATIBILITY_LEVEL = 120;
GO
USE [AdventureWorks];
SET STATISTICS IO ON;
SET NOCOUNT ON;
GO
```

```
--8-7.1 Query to produce Sequence Project
PRINT '8-7.1';
SELECT CustomerID, ROW_NUMBER() OVER(ORDER BY SalesOrderID) AS RowNumber
FROM Sales.SalesOrderHeader;

--8-7.2 A query to show the Sort operator
PRINT '8-7.2';
SELECT CustomerID, SalesOrderID,
    ROW_NUMBER() OVER(PARTITION BY CustomerID ORDER BY OrderDate) AS RowNumber
FROM Sales.SalesOrderHeader;

--8-7.3 A query with a Table Spool operator
PRINT '8-7.3';
SELECT CustomerID, SalesOrderID, SUM(TotalDue) OVER(PARTITION BY CustomerID)
    AS SubTotal
FROM Sales.SalesOrderHeader;
```

Figure 8-8 shows the results from the Messages tab produced by the STATISTICS IO setting. The listing begins by turning on STATISTICS IO and turning off row counts. Before each query, a PRINT statement prints the query number so that you will know which information goes with which query.

```
8-7.1
Table 'SalesOrderHeader'. Scan count 1, logical reads 689, physical reads
8-7.2
Table 'Worktable'. Scan count 0, logical reads 0, physical reads 0, read-al
Table 'SalesOrderHeader'. Scan count 1, logical reads 689, physical reads
8-7.3
Table 'Worktable'. Scan count 3, logical reads 139407, physical reads 0, r
Table 'SalesOrderHeader'. Scan count 1, logical reads 689, physical reads
```

Figure 8-8. *The STATISTICS IO output from the queries*

The most useful information comes from *logical reads,* which is the number of pages read. Query 1 and Query 2 each take 689 logical reads. That is approximately the number of pages in the clustered index of the Sales.SalesOrderHeader table. If you look back at Figure 8-1, you will see that a clustered index scan was performed. Query 3 with a window aggregate takes 689 logical reads to scan the clustered index, but it also creates a worktable in tempdb. It uses 139,407 logical reads to perform the calculations using the worktable.

Using STATISTICS IO can be very beneficial in cases where the execution plans show identical costs, but the queries take a different amount of time to run. I always use both tools when I am tuning queries.

Indexing to Improve the Performance of Window Functions

Sorting is often the bottleneck in queries with window functions. You saw the Sort operator take 95% of the resources in the query from Listing 8-4. It is possible, by adding the correct index, to eliminate the sort and decrease the logical reads. The optimum index will sort correctly and cover the query. Of course, you can't add an index for every query you write, but for queries where the performance is critical, you will know what to do.

Rerun the query from Listing 8-4, making sure the actual execution plan setting is toggled on first. Click the Select operator and view the tooltip, as shown in Figure 8-9. You can see a Memory Grant of 4416 reserved as space for sorting and the Estimated Subtree Cost of 2.71698.

Figure 8-9. *The SELECT tooltip*

Click the Sort operator and then press F4 to see the properties. The Order By property lists two columns. Figure 8-10 shows the information.

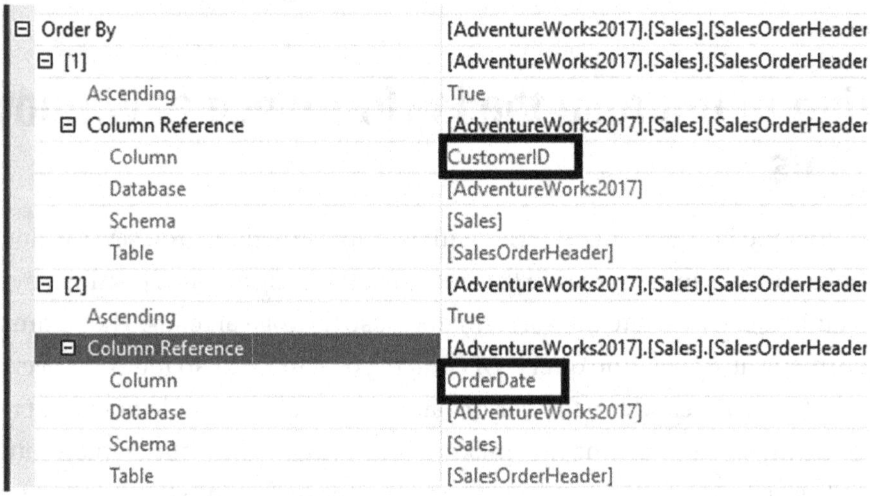

Figure 8-10. *The Order By columns*

The Sort operator is sorting by CustomerID and OrderDate. This makes sense because the PARTITION BY expression is CustomerID and the ORDER BY expression is OrderDate. The data had to be divided by the PARTITION BY column and then sorted by the ORDER BY column. Notice also in the figure that there are three Output List columns. If you look at the Output List, you will see CustomerID, OrderDate, and SaleOrderID, the three columns used in the query. The candidate index will have CustomerID and OrderDate as the keys and SalesOrderID as an included column. In this case, SalesOrderID is not required since it is the cluster key of the table and it is already part of any nonclustered index.

Another thing to consider is existing indexes on the table. The table has a nonclustered index on CustomerID, IX_SalesOrderHeader_CustomerID. Instead of creating a new index, you can modify this one. Queries that previously used the old index can now use the new one. Run Listing 8-8 to drop the existing index and create a new one.

Listing 8-8. Modifying the Index

```
--8-8.1 Drop the existing index
DROP INDEX [IX_SalesOrderHeader_CustomerID] ON [Sales].[SalesOrderHeader];
GO
```

```
--8-8.2 Create a new index for the query
CREATE NONCLUSTERED INDEX [IX_SalesOrderHeader_CustomerID_OrderDate]
   ON [Sales].[SalesOrderHeader] ([CustomerID], [OrderDate]);
```

Now rerun the query from Listing 8-4. The new execution plan is shown in Figure 8-11.

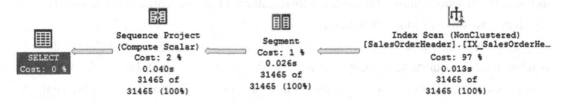

Figure 8-11. *The execution plan after the index change*

The first thing you should see is that the Sort operator is gone. Now the main cost of running the query is scanning the new nonclustered index. Figure 8-12 shows the SELECT tooltip.

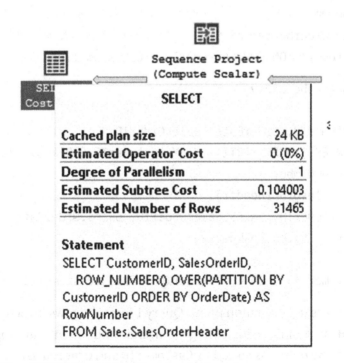

Figure 8-12. *The SELECT tooltip after the index change*

The Memory Grant is no longer needed, and the Estimated Subtree Cost is just 0.104003. That's quite an improvement! In the case of a query with a WHERE clause, add the column to the index in the first position before the PARTITION BY and OVER columns. In the preceding example, it would make sense to create a new index instead of adding to the index starting with CustomerID so that existing queries that needed CustomerID as the first key would not be affected. Unfortunately, if the new column is not part of the OVER clause, the sort may come back.

An index designed this way works well to improve performance for any single table window function query. Most queries, however, have more than one table. Listing 8-9 shows two ways to return the same results from a multi-table query. The queries have different execution plans. The outcome assumes that the index change from Listing 8-8 was made.

Listing 8-9. Window Functions with Joins

```
--8-9.1 query with a join
SELECT SOH.CustomerID, SOH.SalesOrderID, SOH.OrderDate, C.TerritoryID,
    ROW_NUMBER() OVER(PARTITION BY SOH.CustomerID ORDER BY SOH.OrderDate)
        AS RowNumber
FROM Sales.SalesOrderHeader AS SOH
JOIN Sales.Customer C ON SOH.CustomerID = C.CustomerID;

--8-9.2 Rearrange the query
WITH Sales AS (
    SELECT CustomerID, OrderDate, SalesOrderID,
        ROW_NUMBER() OVER(PARTITION BY CustomerID ORDER BY OrderDate)
            AS RowNumber
    FROM Sales.SalesOrderHeader)
SELECT Sales.CustomerID, SALES.SalesOrderID, Sales.OrderDate,
    C.TerritoryID, Sales.RowNumber
FROM Sales
JOIN Sales.Customer AS C ON C.CustomerID = Sales.CustomerID;
```

Figure 8-13 shows the execution plans. Query 1 joins the rows from the Customer and SalesOrderHeader tables with a Merge Join since both indexes are sorted on CustomerID. Then the output is sorted by CustomerID and OrderDate and the row number is calculated. Query 2 moves the SalesOrderHeader table to a CTE and applies the row number there. You can see from the execution plan that the row number is applied before joining to the Customer table. You can also see that the Sort is gone, and the relative cost is 12%. In this case, by rearranging the query, the second query performed better. Both the PARTITION BY and ORDER BY columns are from the same query, but that is not always the case. Queries become complex very quickly, and you may not always be able to eliminate sorting. I have seen situations involving queries with several joined tables that had a stubborn Sort operator that I was not able to remove. Fortunately, the cost of the sorting was usually small in comparison to other operators in the plan.

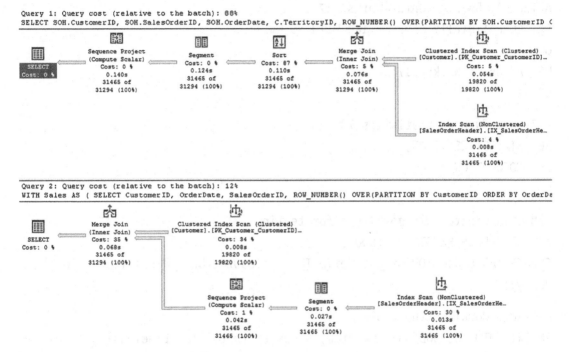

Figure 8-13. *The execution plans for a join*

Framing for Performance

In Chapter 5, you learned about adding a frame to the OVER clause to create moving aggregates. In Chapter 6, you saw how the frame is needed for the FIRST_VALUE and LAST_VALUE functions. In each case, I explained that the frame was sometimes needed to get the correct results, but it's also important for performance reasons. Later in the chapter, I'll cover some exciting performance updates with SQL Server 2019, but for now, the examples in this section will assume that the database is in SQL Server 2017 compatibility mode or lower.

If the tables are small, the queries run quickly even if the frame is left out. Listing 8-10 sets the database compatibility mode to 2017 (140) and turns on statistics. It then creates and populates a table for testing. If needed, modify the database name.

Listing 8-10. Create a Large Test Table

```
--8-10.1 Set the compatibility level
USE master;
GO
ALTER DATABASE AdventureWorks2017
SET COMPATIBILITY_LEVEL = 140 WITH NO_WAIT;
GO
USE AdventureWorks2017;
GO

--8-10.2 Turn on Statistics IO
SET STATISTICS IO ON;
SET NOCOUNT ON;
GO

--8-10.3 Create a larger table for testing
DROP TABLE IF EXISTS dbo.SOD ;
CREATE TABLE dbo.SOD(SalesOrderID INT, SalesOrderDetailID INT, LineTotal
Money);

--8-10.4 Populate the table
INSERT INTO dbo.SOD(SalesOrderID, SalesOrderDetailID, LineTotal)
SELECT SalesOrderID, SalesOrderDetailID, LineTotal
FROM Sales.SalesOrderDetail
UNION ALL
SELECT SalesOrderID + MAX(SalesOrderID) OVER(), SalesOrderDetailID,
LineTotal
FROM Sales.SalesOrderDetail;

--8-10.5 Create a nonclustered index
CREATE INDEX SalesOrderID_SOD ON dbo.SOD
(SalesOrderID, SalesOrderDetailID) INCLUDE(LineTotal);
```

Listing 8-11 contains two queries that don't perform well. Be sure to toggle on the actual execution plan before running the script.

Listing 8-11. Two Queries with Poor Performance

```
--8-11.1 A running total
PRINT '8-11.1'
SELECT SalesOrderID, SalesOrderDetailID, LineTotal,
    SUM(LineTotal)
    OVER(PARTITION BY SalesOrderID ORDER BY SalesOrderDetailID) RunningTotal
FROM SOD;

--8-11.2 A query with FIRST_VALUE
PRINT '8-11.2'
SELECT SalesOrderID, SalesOrderDetailID, LineTotal,
    FIRST_VALUE(LineTotal)
    OVER(PARTITION BY SalesOrderID ORDER BY SalesOrderDetailID) FirstValue
FROM SOD;
```

Figure 8-14 shows the statistics information. In each case, over 1.4 million logical reads were taken from a worktable.

```
8-10.1
Table 'Worktable'. Scan count 305564, logical reads 1455804, physical reads 0,
Table 'SOD'. Scan count 1, logical reads 908, physical reads 0, read-ahead rea
8-10.2
Table 'Worktable'. Scan count 305564, logical reads 1455804, physical reads 0,
Table 'SOD'. Scan count 1, logical reads 908, physical reads 0, read-ahead rea
```

Figure 8-14. *The logical reads from two poorly performing queries*

Figure 8-15 shows the execution plans for the queries. Note the Window Spool operator that shows that a worktable was created, but it was not created in memory.

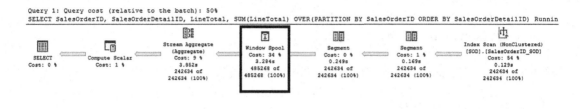

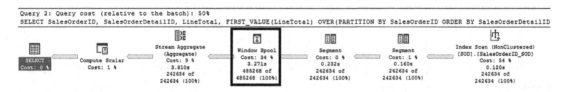

Figure 8-15. *The execution plans for two poorly performing queries*

When framing is support but left out, the default frame is used. The default frame is
RANGE BETWEEN UNBOUNDED PRECEEDING AND CURRENT ROW. The RANGE operator is meant
for logical time periods which hasn't been implemented in SQL Server. When RANGE is
used, the worktable is always created in tempdb, not memory. To get around this issue,
specify the ROWS operator in the frame. Listing 8-12 shows the corrected queries.

Listing 8-12. Queries with ROWS

```
PRINT '8-12.1'
SELECT SalesOrderID, SalesOrderDetailID, LineTotal,
    SUM(LineTotal)
        OVER(PARTITION BY SalesOrderID ORDER BY SalesOrderDetailID
        ROWS BETWEEN UNBOUNDED PRECEDING AND CURRENT ROW) RunningTotal
FROM SOD;

--8-12.2 A query with FIRST_VALUE using ROWS
PRINT '8-12.2'
SELECT SalesOrderID, SalesOrderDetailID, LineTotal,
        FIRST_VALUE(LineTotal)
        OVER(PARTITION BY SalesOrderID ORDER BY SalesOrderDetailID
        ROWS BETWEEN UNBOUNDED PRECEDING AND CURRENT ROW) RunningTotal
FROM SOD;
```

Figure 8-16 shows that the worktables now take 0 logical reads. This shows you that
the worktables are created in memory. If you review the execution plans, they will be
identical to the plans shown in Figure 8-15.

```
8-11.1
Table 'Worktable'. Scan count 0, logical reads 0, physical reads 0,
Table 'SOD'. Scan count 1, logical reads 908, physical reads 0, read
8-11.2
Table 'Worktable'. Scan count 0, logical reads 0, physical reads 0,
Table 'SOD'. Scan count 1, logical reads 908, physical reads 0, read
```

Figure 8-16. *The logical reads when using ROWS*

These examples compared the logical reads, but how do you know that this really makes a difference in how long the queries take to run? If your customer calls to complain about a slowly running query, explaining that the logical reads look good will mean nothing to them. In the "Measuring Time Comparisons" section of this chapter, you'll see that there really is a performance difference suggested by the logical reads.

Taking Advantage of Batch Mode on Rowstore

There are two types of window functions that have not scaled well in the past: window aggregates and statistical functions. These functions are easy to use, but performance suffers if operating on a large number of rows. You can get around these issues by pre-aggregating so that the functions are applied to a smaller number of rows, but this is not always possible. Listing 8-13 shows two examples using the table created in Listing 8-10 and making sure that the database is in 2017 (140) compatibility mode.

Listing 8-13. A Window Aggregate and a Statistical Function

```
--8-13.1 Set the compatibility level
USE master;
GO
ALTER DATABASE AdventureWorks2017
SET COMPATIBILITY_LEVEL = 140 WITH NO_WAIT;
GO
USE AdventureWorks2017;
GO
--8-13.2 A window aggregate
PRINT '8-13.1'
```

```
SELECT SalesOrderID, SalesOrderDetailID, LineTotal,
    SUM(LineTotal) OVER(PARTITION BY SalesOrderID) AS SubTotal
FROM SOD;

--8-13.2 A statistical function
PRINT '8-11.2'
SELECT SalesOrderID, SalesOrderDetailID, LineTotal,
        PERCENT_RANK()
        OVER(PARTITION BY SalesOrderID ORDER BY SalesOrderDetailID) AS
        Ranking
FROM SOD;
```

Figure 8-17 shows the logical reads. Notice that there are a large number of logical reads due to worktables.

```
8-12.1
Table 'Worktable'. Scan count 3, logical reads 736989, physical reads 0,
Table 'SOD'. Scan count 1, logical reads 908, physical reads 0, read-ahe
8-11.2
Table 'Worktable'. Scan count 3, logical reads 736989, physical reads 0,
Table 'SOD'. Scan count 1, logical reads 908, physical reads 0, read-ahe
```

Figure 8-17. *The logical reads from a window aggregate and a statistical function*

The actual execution plans are quite complex despite the simple query syntax. Figure 8-18 shows the partial plans. Note that each has more than one Table Spool operator. Table Spool operators mean that the worktable is created in tempdb. It will always take a lot of resources even though the estimated cost is low.

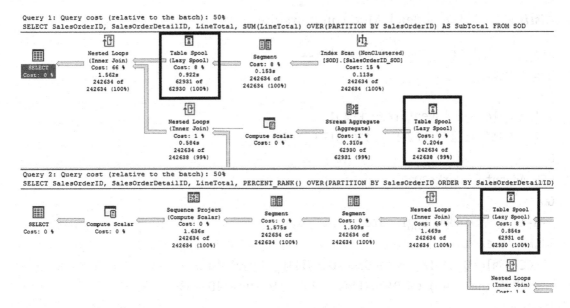

Figure 8-18. *The execution plans showing Table Spool operators*

You may be wondering why the PERCENT_RANK function has poor performance when the RANK function's performance is acceptable. This is because the formula for the PERCENT_RANK function is (RANK -1)/(TotalRows -1). Under the covers, the window aggregate COUNT is used to calculate the total rows. The other three statistical functions suffer from the same performance issues as well.

In 2012, Microsoft introduced nonclustered Columnstore Indexes (CI). CIs are a different way to store data where a page contains one column of many, possibly thousands, of rows. This means that high levels of compression are possible, and queries can be faster by an order of magnitude. With each version of SQL Server, Microsoft has enhanced CI, including a new way to process aggregates on large data sets, Batch Mode. This is especially useful for queries that require high CPU resources. Before SQL Server 2019 (still in preview at the time of this writing), a CI had to be involved in the query. Starting with 2019, the optimizer can choose to use Batch Mode even when no CI is part of the query. This is called Batch Mode on Rowstore.

Listing 8-14 demonstrates how the new Batch Mode on Rowstore improves the performance of a window aggregate query.

Listing 8-14. Using Batch Mode on Rowstore

```
--8-14.1 Set the compatibility level
USE master;
GO
ALTER DATABASE AdventureWorks2017
SET COMPATIBILITY_LEVEL = 150 WITH NO_WAIT;
GO
USE AdventureWorks2017;
GO
--8-14.2 A window aggregate
PRINT '8-14.1'
SELECT SalesOrderID, SalesOrderDetailID, LineTotal,
    SUM(LineTotal) OVER(PARTITION BY SalesOrderID) AS SubTotal
FROM SOD;
```

Figure 8-19 shows the logical reads. Notice that there are 0 logical reads for the worktable.

```
8-13.1
Table 'SOD'. Scan count 1, logical reads 908, physical reads 0, read
Table 'Worktable'. Scan count 0, logical reads 0, physical reads 0,
```

Figure 8-19. *The logical reads when Batch Mode is used*

Figure 8-20 shows the actual execution plan. In this case, the plan is quite simple compared to running the same query when in 2017 compatibility. Notice also that a new operator, the Window Aggregate operator, is part of the plan.

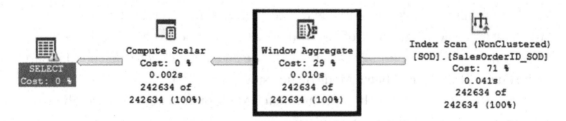

Figure 8-20. *The plan with the Window Aggregate operator*

When you hover over the operator, you'll see the properties shown in Figure 8-21. Notice that the Execution Mode is Batch.

```
: to the batch
lerDetailID, L
```

Window Aggregate	
Computes values of functions across the windows defined by the OVER clause. Input rowset is suitably sorted stream.	
Physical Operation	Window Aggregate
Actual Execution Mode	Batch
Estimated Execution Mode	Batch
Actual Number of Rows	242634
Actual Number of Batches	270
Estimated Operator Cost	0.380933 (29%)
Estimated I/O Cost	0
Estimated CPU Cost	0.380935
Estimated Subtree Cost	1.31852
Number of Executions	1
Estimated Number of Executions	1
Estimated Number of Rows	242634
Estimated Row Size	39 B
Actual Rebinds	0
Actual Rewinds	0
Node ID	1

Output List
[AdventureWorks2017].[dbo].[SOD].SalesOrderID,
[AdventureWorks2017].[dbo].[SOD].SalesOrderDetailID,
[AdventureWorks2017].[dbo].[SOD].LineTotal, Expr1004,
Expr1005

Figure 8-21. *Batch execution mode*

Over the years since window aggregates have been introduced, I have loved using them, but I was always concerned about performance. Now, when the function must operate over a large number of rows, Batch Mode can kick in and improve the performance. Note that Microsoft doesn't publish when it's worth it to switch to Batch Mode, so your results will vary.

Batch Mode on Rowstore also helps the performance of the statistical functions, PERCENT_RANK, CUME_DIST, PERCENTILE_CONT, and PERCENTILE_DISC. Under the hood, these functions use window aggregates in their formulas, so it makes sense that they would benefit.

At the time of this writing, there is no word on which editions of SQL Server will include this great feature.

Measuring Time Comparisons

So far you have learned what to look for in the execution plan and STATISTICS IO. Your customer, however, will not care about the execution plan or the logical reads. Your customer only cares about how fast the query runs. Another setting called STATISTICS TIME can be used to measure how long a query takes to run. While STATISTICS IO is beneficial to compare the IO between two queries, you may also be interested in how long the queries actually run especially when working with longer running queries. Listing 8-15 shows an example using the dbo.SOD table created earlier in the chapter.

Listing 8-15. Using STATISTICS TIME

```
--8-15.1 Change settings
SET STATISTICS IO OFF;
SET STATISTICS TIME ON;
GO
--8-15.2 Change compatibility
USE MASTER;
GO
ALTER DATABASE AdventureWorks2017
SET COMPATIBILITY_LEVEL = 140 WITH NO_WAIT;
USE AdventureWorks2017;
GO
--8-15.3
PRINT '
DEFAULT frame'
SELECT SalesOrderID, SalesOrderDetailID, LineTotal,
    SUM(LineTotal) OVER(PARTITION BY SalesOrderID
        ORDER BY SalesOrderDetailID) AS RunningTotal
FROM SOD;

--8-15.4
PRINT '
ROWS'
```

```
SELECT SalesOrderID, SalesOrderDetailID, LineTotal,
    SUM(LineTotal) OVER(PARTITION BY SalesOrderID
        ORDER BY SalesOrderDetailID
        ROWS BETWEEN UNBOUNDED PRECEDING AND CURRENT ROW) AS SubTotal
FROM SOD;
```

The listing compares two queries that return running totals. The first using the default frame, and the second uses ROWS. The compatibility mode was also changed to SQL Server 2017 as to not take advantage of batch mode. Figure 8-22 shows the information returned by STATISTICS TIME.

```
DEFAULT frame

  SQL Server Execution Times:
    CPU time = 0 ms,   elapsed time = 0 ms.

(242634 rows affected)

  SQL Server Execution Times:
    CPU time = 21579 ms,   elapsed time = 21649 ms.

ROWS

  SQL Server Execution Times:
    CPU time = 0 ms,   elapsed time = 0 ms.

(242634 rows affected)

  SQL Server Execution Times:
    CPU time = 1718 ms,   elapsed time = 1910 ms.
```

Figure 8-22. *The STATISTICS TIME information*

Using ROWS took less than 2 seconds, while leaving out the frame took about 21 seconds. There are several other ways to time the amount of time a query takes to run. You can run an Extended Events session, for example. One other thing to keep in mind if you do time the queries using the Query Window is that the time to populate the grid is also included. You can also turn on *Discard results after execution* in the SSMS options to avoid populating the grid. This setting also affected the Messages tab in some earlier versions of SSMS. To avoid any issues with this, Listing 8-16 throws the rows into temp tables instead of displaying them.

Listing 8-16. Throwing the rows away

```
--8-16.1
PRINT '
DEFAULT frame'
SELECT SalesOrderID, SalesOrderDetailID, LineTotal,
    SUM(LineTotal) OVER(PARTITION BY SalesOrderID
        ORDER BY SalesOrderDetailID) AS RunningTotal
INTO #temp1
FROM SOD;

--8-16.2
PRINT '
ROWS'
SELECT SalesOrderID, SalesOrderDetailID, LineTotal,
    SUM(LineTotal) OVER(PARTITION BY SalesOrderID
        ORDER BY SalesOrderDetailID
        ROWS BETWEEN UNBOUNDED PRECEDING AND CURRENT ROW) AS SubTotal
INTO #Temp2
FROM SOD;

DROP TABLE #Temp1;
DROP TABLE #temp2;
```

Figure 8-23 shows the difference.

```
DEFAULT frame

 SQL Server Execution Times:
   CPU time = 0 ms,  elapsed time = 0 ms.

 SQL Server Execution Times:
   CPU time = 26811 ms,  elapsed time = 7095 ms.

(242634 rows affected)

ROWS

 SQL Server Execution Times:
   CPU time = 0 ms,  elapsed time = 0 ms.

 SQL Server Execution Times:
   CPU time = 2143 ms,  elapsed time = 809 ms.

(242634 rows affected)
```

Figure 8-23. *The time when throwing away the results*

Note   You may notice something strange. Why is the CPU time greater than the elapsed time? This is because the optimizer divided the query over multiple cores with parallelism, so the time is the sum over all the cores.

I find it interesting to perform comparisons over an even larger number of rows. To do so, I've run a script from data platform guru, Adam Machanic, called Thinking Big Adventure. (You can easily find this script by Googling for it.) This script creates a 30-million-row table called bigTransactionHistory. If you are interested in running timings yourself, the queries used will be available along with the other queries in this chapter.

Figure 8-24 compares using a window aggregate to a CTE producing the same results. When running in 2016 mode on my VM, it took 5 minutes to run the window aggregate compared to 1.75 minutes when using a CTE. Both methods ran fast when switching to 2019.

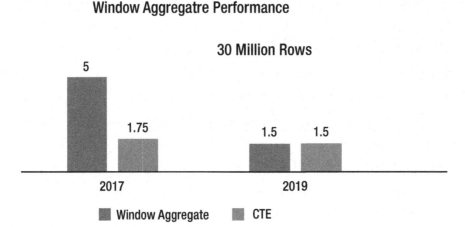

Figure 8-24. *Window aggregate performance*

Figure 8-25 shows the difference for running totals between the default frame and ROWS. With 2016, it took 36 minutes when using the default frame compared to 3.5 minutes with ROWS. Switching to 2019 mode took only 1.3 minutes for each!

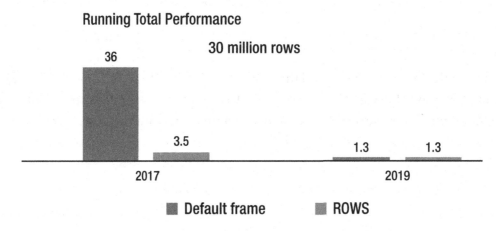

Figure 8-25. *Running total performance*

Cleaning Up the Database

If you would like to return your AdventureWorks database back to its original state, you can run Listing 8-17.

Listing 8-17. Cleaning Up the Database

```
--8-17.1 Drop index
DROP INDEX [IX_SalesOrderHeader_CustomerID_OrderDate]
    ON Sales.SalesOrderHeader;
GO

--8-17-2 Recreate original index
CREATE INDEX [IX_SalesOrderHeader_CustomerID] ON Sales.SalesOrderHeader
    (CustomerID);

--8-17-3 Drop special table
DROP TABLE IF EXISTS dbo.SOD;
--8-17-4 Drop Thinking Big Adventure tables
DROP TABLE IF EXISTS dbo.bigTransactionHistory;
DROP TABLE IF EXISTS dbo.bigProduct;
```

Summary

You can affect the performance of queries with window functions by adding an index that sorts on the PARTITION BY and ORDER BY clauses. A properly constructed index can improve the performance of many queries containing window functions. When the frame is supported, it's important to include it. In some cases, you can also take advantage of the 2019 Batch Mode on Rowstore feature.

Now that you understand all the possible types of window functions available and how to tune them, it's time to see even more real-world examples. In Chapter 9, you'll play with baseball data!

Hitting a Home Run with Gaps, Islands, and Streaks

Within any set of data, we may examine how that data groups together. This can allow us to identify missing rows, find unusual patterns, or develop advanced analytical techniques. At its simplest, being able to locate gaps and islands will tell us about missing data values. As we delve deeper, it will allow us to identify streaks, droughts, or anomalous events worthy of further investigation.

At the core of this idea are boundaries. A boundary represents a stopping point or transition where statistically significant sets of data meet. Dates and times are the most common natural boundary conditions found in data as so much of our world is organized by when events occur. We can also look at ranges of identity values and determine when a value is missing or how many sequential values exist before a gap is found. Any data that can be meaningfully sorted can be analyzed for the existence of gaps, islands, or data groups.

To effectively demonstrate these concepts and techniques, we will use a set of baseball data for our work. Because baseball is an old sport and our data spans over a hundred years, it makes for an excellent set of test data as it is large, messy, and full of unusual events. Databases in 1920 were not up to par with what we have today, so we can be assured that there exist bad, missing, or unusual events that will make for fun analytics.

Window functions are essential for performing gaps/islands analysis as they provide immense flexibility and allow us to apply complex analytics without the need for pages of T-SQL. While correlated subqueries, temporary tables, or iteration can be used, our goal will be to present solutions that are easy to read and maintain and that perform reasonably well.

141

© Kathi Kellenberger, Clayton Groom, and Ed Pollack 2019
K. Kellenberger et al., *Expert T-SQL Window Functions in SQL Server 2019*,
https://doi.org/10.1007/978-1-4842-5197-3_9

The Classic Gaps/Islands Problem

For our analysis in this chapter, we will define a gap as the distance between the end of one sequence and the beginning of the next. An island is the data set bounded by the end of a previous gap and the start of the next. Both gaps and islands are defined by a range of values that indicate the beginning of a gap or island and the end of that gap or island. Gaps and islands coexist and the presence of one implies that of the other. A gap may not exist without islands of data surrounding it, and an island may not exist without gaps surrounding it. The beginning and end of a data set will often be treated as terminators and act similarly to gaps, even if we do not consider them gaps in our data.

A gap is the distance between two sequences of data, whereas an island is the data bounded by a pair of gaps.

The simplest application of gaps analysis is to look for missing ID values within a table. Consider a table that we populate with a set of integers, as seen in Listing 9-1.

Listing 9-1. Create and Populate a Table of Integer Values for Gaps Analysis

```
CREATE TABLE dbo.integers
       (integer_id INT NOT NULL);

INSERT INTO dbo.integers
       (integer_id)
VALUES
       (1), (2), (3), (4), (5), (6), (7), (8), (9), (12), (13), (14),
       (15), (17), (19), (20), (21), (22), (23), (24);
```

We intentionally skip some values in the INSERT statement. The challenge is to determine the best way to locate the missing integer values using TSQL. Since this is a small list, we can visually confirm the missing values in our INSERT:

1 2 3 4 5 6 7 8 9...12 13 14 15...17...19 20 21 22 23 24

The simplest and slowest way to do this would be to iterate through the table, count integers one by one, and flag any missing values when they are encountered. This is easy to understand, but dreadfully slow and limited. In a more realistic data set with millions or billions of rows, iterating through every value to find missing data would be inefficient

142

enough as to not be worth the effort. Furthermore, that strategy would fail against noninteger data, such as dates and times. For these data types, the distance between values is indeterminate and additional analysis is required to define gaps and islands.

Finding Islands

Window functions allow us to process this data in a single step and return a list of results, as seen in Listing 9-2.

Listing 9-2. Query to Return Islands Within a Nonrepeating Integer List

```
WITH CTE_ISLANDS AS (
        SELECT
                integer_id,
                integer_id - ROW_NUMBER() OVER (ORDER BY integer_id) AS
                gap_quantity
        FROM dbo.integers)
SELECT
        MIN(integer_id) AS island_start,
        MAX(integer_id) AS island_end
FROM CTE_ISLANDS
GROUP BY gap_quantity;
```

In this query, we define a common-table expression that returns the integer value, as well as the difference between that value and its row number. In a nonrepeating sequence of positive integers, that difference can only be accounted for by a gap in the sequence, for which we can use MIN and MAX to quantify the endpoints of the remaining islands of data. The results can be seen in Figure 9-1.

	island_start	island_end
1	1	9
2	12	15
3	17	17
4	19	24

Figure 9-1. *Islands of integers found via the query in Listing 9-2*

Dealing with duplicates is important, so we'll continue our analysis by adding some duplicates to our integer list:

```
INSERT INTO dbo.integers
        (integer_id)
VALUES
        (2), (12), (12), (24);
```

If we run our previous query, the results shown in Figure 9-2 will appear to be nonsense.

Figure 9-2. *Islands of integers found via the query in Listing 9-2*

The presence of duplicates throws off our calculations, as they are based on the assumption that row counts indicate distinct values. The window function DENSE_RANK can solve this problem for us as it considers only distinct values and will not issue multiple IDs to duplicates. Listing 9-3 shows a new query that uses this window function to provide an accurate list of islands.

Listing 9-3. Using DENSE_RANK to Account for Duplicate Values

```
WITH CTE_ISLANDS AS (
        SELECT
                integer_id,
                integer_id - DENSE_RANK() OVER (ORDER BY integer_id) AS
                gap_quantity
        FROM dbo.integers)
SELECT
        MIN(integer_id) AS island_start,
        MAX(integer_id) AS island_end,
        COUNT(*) AS distinct_value_count
FROM CTE_ISLANDS
GROUP BY gap_quantity;
```

144

The results of this query confirm that we can return the set of islands even in the presence of duplicates, as seen in Figure 9-3.

	island_start	island_end	distinct_value_count
1	1	9	10
2	12	15	6
3	17	17	1
4	19	24	7

Figure 9-3. *Islands of integers found via the query in Listing 9-2*

As a bonus, we have included the count of rows within each island. This is valuable as it does include duplicates. The range of 1-9 includes 10 values since the number 2 is repeated once. This can be useful for quantifying the volume of data within a given island, regardless of specific values. If we wanted to return the absolute island length ignoring duplicate values, we could simply subtract the island starting value from the ending value and add 1. For example, 9-1 + 1 = 9 distinct integer values within the range 1-9.

Finding Gaps

Locating gaps in data requires us to consider the set of islands first and then invert that data set to find the gaps in between them. This requires a bit more work but can be accomplished in a similar fashion as locating islands. The query in Listing 9-4 shows one method for finding gaps within a list of integers.

Listing 9-4. Finding Gaps via a Self-Joining CTE Using ROW_NUMBER

```
WITH CTE_GAPS AS (
    SELECT
            integer_id,
            ROW_NUMBER() OVER (ORDER BY integer_id) AS island_quantity
    FROM dbo.integers)
SELECT
        ISLAND_END.integer_id + 1 AS gap_starting_value,
        ISLAND_START.integer_id - 1 AS gap_ending_value,
        ISLAND_START.integer_id - ISLAND_END.integer_id - 1 AS gap_length
```

```
FROM CTE_GAPS AS ISLAND_END
INNER JOIN CTE_GAPS AS ISLAND_START
ON ISLAND_START.island_quantity = ISLAND_END.island_quantity + 1
WHERE ISLAND_START.integer_id - ISLAND_END.integer_id > 1;
```

The results of this query can be found in Figure 9-4 and provide the three gaps present in our set of integers.

	gap_starting_value	gap_ending_value	gap_length
1	10	11	2
2	16	16	1
3	18	18	1

Figure 9-4. *Gaps within a set of integers, including the gap length*

The results show us three gaps that fit within the four islands identified earlier. Since gaps are defined as an absence of values, the gap length is simply the number of integers within the range. Similarly, repeated values have no bearing on our results and we intentionally use ROW_NUMBER instead of DENSE_RANK as counting duplicates would throw off our gap calculations and result in bad ranges whenever duplicates were present.

Limitations and Notes

The number of islands in a data set will always equal the number of gaps plus one. While this may seem like a trivial fact, it allows us to make simplifying assumptions about how gaps and islands relate to each other and assign a pair of islands to each gap as being related to it. In a discussion of data proximity, the events that occur immediately before and after a gap may be significant, and assigning them special meaning may allow for the prediction of future events. If a gap or island represents an anomaly and we can uniquely quantify the events leading up to it as the corresponding gap or island, then those events can be alerted on and potentially avoided using automation.

There are many ways to return gaps and islands within a set of data. We will standardize on those that are the easiest to write, document, and maintain. A discussion of performance will occur later in this chapter and will address ways to speed up gaps/islands analytics in the event that latency or resource consumption concerns.

So far, our examples have centered around a set of positive integers. While we have acknowledged repeated values, our analysis will not work on other data types. If we wished to find gaps or islands within a set of decimals, dates, or times, our calculations would be insufficient. The remainder of this chapter will center on extending gaps and islands analysis to encompass data that we would encounter in the real world. This data will often be crunched by analyzing dates and times, rather than integers or identities, and will require additional code to do so meaningfully.

Data Clusters

Real data rarely consists of sequential nonrepeating positive integers. While IDs are often used to organize information, it is typically dates and times that are used to naturally reference it. Performing gaps and islands analysis against data based on datetime components leads us into defining a new entity: a data cluster.

Data can be grouped based on boundaries that we create. For example, we can take sales data and group it by month, fiscal quarter, or year in order to view changes over time. These groupings are static and unchanging. We know that a quarterly report will contain 4 buckets of data per year, a monthly report will contain 12, and a weekly report will contain 52.

We can choose to group data organically as well, creating rules and allowing data to be partitioned into an unknown number of segments based on those rules. The rules we choose will be based on a measure of proximity and will determine whether two events are related to each other by checking if they are within the same data island as each other.

A data cluster is an organically grouped set of data that is represented by a single island within a larger data set. The dimension used to determine grouping rules may be numeric, such as an integer or decimal, or it may be a datetime. In theory, any data type may be used for this purpose so long as we can construct rules about how the data interacts. For example, word strings could be used in determining data clusters if proximity happened to be calculated based on alphabetical distance.

To introduce this concept, let's consider the plight of the on-call technician. Alerts are received when things break; the technician wakes up and fixes them, heads back to bed, and sleeps until the next thing breaks. When looking back on alerts from the past week or month or year, there would be value in grouping events by those that are most likely related.

The easiest way to do so is to look at timing. Events that occur close together in time are likely (though not guaranteed) to be related. If a network switch breaks, then everything attached to it becomes unreachable. If a cloud service becomes unavailable for a minute, then any application that uses that service will also encounter trouble.

Let's build a simple set of data to introduce this concept. Listing 9-5 shows the TSQL to create a new table and populate it with test data.

Listing 9-5. Create an Error Log for Demonstration of Simple Data Cluster/Proximity Analytics

```
CREATE TABLE dbo.error_log
(          error_log_id INT NOT NULL IDENTITY(1,1) CONSTRAINT PK_error_log
           PRIMARY KEY CLUSTERED,
        error_time_utc DATETIME NOT NULL,
        error_source VARCHAR(50) NOT NULL,
        severity VARCHAR(10) NOT NULL,
        error_description VARCHAR(100) NOT NULL);
GO

INSERT INTO dbo.error_log (error_time_utc, error_source, severity, error_
description)
VALUES
        ('2/20/2019 00:00:15', 'print_server_01', 'low', 'device unreachable'),
        ('2/21/2019 00:00:13', 'print_server_01', 'low', 'device unreachable'),
        ('2/22/2019 00:00:11', 'print_server_01', 'low', 'device unreachable'),
        ('2/23/2019 00:00:17', 'print_server_01', 'low', 'device unreachable'),
        ('2/24/2019 00:00:12', 'print_server_01', 'low', 'device unreachable'),
        ('2/25/2019 00:00:15', 'print_server_01', 'low', 'device unreachable'),
        ('2/26/2019 00:00:12', 'print_server_01', 'low', 'device unreachable'),
        ('2/22/2019 22:34:01', 'network_switch_05', 'critical', 'device
        unresponsive'),
        ('2/22/2019 22:34:06', 'sql_server_02', 'critical', 'device unreachable'),
        ('2/22/2019 22:34:06', 'sql_server_02 sql service', 'critical',
        'service down'),
        ('2/22/2019 22:34:06', 'sql_server_02 sql server agent service',
        'high', 'service down'),
        ('2/22/2019 22:34:06', 'app_server_11', 'critical', 'device unreachable'),
        ('2/22/2019 22:34:11', 'file_server_03', 'high', 'device unreachable'),
        ('2/22/2019 22:34:31', 'app_server_10', 'critical', 'device unreachable'),
        ('2/22/2019 22:34:39', 'web_server', 'medium', 'device unreachable'),
        ('2/22/2019 22:35:00', 'web_site', 'medium', 'http 404 thrown'),
```

```
('2/05/2019 03:05:00', 'app_git_repo', 'low', 'repo unavailable'),
('2/12/2019 03:05:00', 'app_git_repo', 'low', 'repo unavailable'),
('2/19/2019 03:05:00', 'app_git_repo', 'low', 'repo unavailable'),
('2/26/2019 03:05:00', 'app_git_repo', 'low', 'repo unavailable'),
('2/26/2019 03:07:15', 'git service error', 'medium', ''),
('1/31/2019 23:59:50', 'sql_server_01', 'critical', 'corrupt
database identified'),
('1/31/2019 23:59:53', 'sql_server_01', 'critical', 'corrupt
database identified'),
('1/31/2019 23:59:57', 'sql_server_01', 'critical', 'corrupt
database identified'),
('2/1/2019 00:00:00', 'sql_server_01 sql service', 'critical',
'service down'),
('2/1/2019 00:00:15', 'sql_server_01 sql server agent service',
'critical', 'service down'),
('2/1/2019 00:15:00', 'etl data load to sql_server_01', 'medium',
'job failed'),
('2/1/2019 00:30:00', 'etl data load to sql_server_01', 'medium',
'job failed'),
('2/1/2019 00:45:00', 'etl data load to sql_server_01', 'medium',
'job failed'),
('2/1/2019 01:00:00', 'etl data load to sql_server_01', 'medium',
'job failed'),
('2/1/2019 01:15:00', 'etl data load to sql_server_01', 'medium',
'job failed'),
('2/1/2019 01:30:00', 'etl data load to sql_server_01', 'medium',
'job failed')
GO
```

A quick select from the table illustrates the sort of data we are working with, as seen in Figure 9-5.

8	28	2019-02-01 01:30:00.000	etl data load to sql_server_01	medium	job failed
9	17	2019-02-05 03:05:00.000	app_git_repo	low	repo unavailable
10	18	2019-02-12 03:05:00.000	app_git_repo	low	repo unavailable
11	19	2019-02-19 03:05:00.000	app_git_repo	low	repo unavailable
12	1	2019-02-20 00:00:15.000	print_server_01	low	device unreachable
13	2	2019-02-21 00:00:13.000	print_server_01	low	device unreachable
14	3	2019-02-22 00:00:11.000	print_server_01	low	device unreachable
15	8	2019-02-22 22:34:01.000	network_switch_05	critical	device unresponsive
16	9	2019-02-22 22:34:06.000	sql_server_02	critical	device unreachable
17	10	2019-02-22 22:34:06.000	sql_server_02 sql service	critical	service down
18	11	2019-02-22 22:34:06.000	sql_server_02 sql server agent service	high	service down
19	12	2019-02-22 22:34:06.000	app_server_11	critical	device unreachable
20	13	2019-02-22 22:34:11.000	file_server_03	high	device unreachable
21	14	2019-02-22 22:34:31.000	app_server_10	critical	device unreachable
22	15	2019-02-22 22:34:39.000	web_server	medium	device unreachable
23	16	2019-02-22 22:35:00.000	web_site	medium	http 404 thrown
24	4	2019-02-23 00:00:17.000	print_server_01	low	device unreachable

Figure 9-5. *Data sample from dbo.error_log*

Our interest is in grouping alerts to show those that relate to each other. This can be done using GROUP BY, but how do we decide what to group by? If an alert occurs at 11:59:59 p.m. and another at 12:00:00 a.m., grouping by date or hour will show these as unrelated events. For our purposes, let's say that all events that occur within 5 minutes of each other are considered part of the same data cluster and are related. Listing 9-6 shows a query that will return errors from the log grouped by this rule.

Listing 9-6. Query to Group Errors into Related Clusters of Data with a Proximity of 5 Minutes

```
WITH CTE_ERROR_HISTORY AS (
        SELECT
                LAG(error_log.error_time_utc) OVER (ORDER BY error_log.
                error_time_utc, error_log.error_log_id) AS previous_event_
                time,
                LEAD(error_log.error_time_utc) OVER (ORDER BY error_log.
                error_time_utc, error_log.error_log_id) AS next_event_time,
                ROW_NUMBER() OVER (ORDER BY error_log.error_time_utc,
                error_log.error_log_id) AS island_location,
```

```
                error_log.error_time_utc,
                error_log.error_log_id
        FROM dbo.error_log),
CTE_ISLAND_START AS (
        SELECT
                ROW_NUMBER() OVER (ORDER BY CTE_ERROR_HISTORY.error_time_
                utc, CTE_ERROR_HISTORY.error_log_id) AS island_number,
                CTE_ERROR_HISTORY.error_time_utc AS island_start_time,
                CTE_ERROR_HISTORY.next_event_time,
                CTE_ERROR_HISTORY.island_location AS island_start_location
        FROM CTE_ERROR_HISTORY
        WHERE DATEDIFF(MINUTE, CTE_ERROR_HISTORY.previous_event_time,
        CTE_ERROR_HISTORY.error_time_utc) > 5 OR CTE_ERROR_HISTORY.
        previous_event_time IS NULL),
CTE_ISLAND_END AS (
        SELECT
                ROW_NUMBER() OVER (ORDER BY CTE_ERROR_HISTORY.error_time_
                utc, CTE_ERROR_HISTORY.error_log_id) AS island_number,
                CTE_ERROR_HISTORY.error_time_utc AS island_end_time,
                CTE_ERROR_HISTORY.next_event_time,
                CTE_ERROR_HISTORY.island_location AS island_end_location
        FROM CTE_ERROR_HISTORY
        WHERE DATEDIFF(MINUTE, CTE_ERROR_HISTORY.error_time_utc, CTE_ERROR_
        HISTORY.next_event_time) > 5 OR CTE_ERROR_HISTORY.next_event_time
        IS NULL)
SELECT
        CTE_ISLAND_START.island_start_time,
        CTE_ISLAND_END.island_end_time,
        CTE_ISLAND_END.island_end_location - CTE_ISLAND_START.island_start_
        location + 1 AS count_of_events
FROM CTE_ISLAND_START
INNER JOIN CTE_ISLAND_END
ON CTE_ISLAND_START.island_number = CTE_ISLAND_END.island_number;
```

This query appears long, but follows a methodical approach that we will adopt for the remainder of our work:

1. Create a rule that determines proximity and when events are related or not.

2. Create a set of data that includes the current event, previous event, and next event.

3. Define the starting points for all data clusters using the proximity rule.

4. Define the ending points for all data clusters using the proximity rule.

5. Join the starting and ending points together to create a result set.

LEAD and LAG are used to quickly retrieve the previous and next events in our data set, whereas ROW_NUMBER is used to track the island count, for joining purposes at the end of our query. The results can be seen in Figure 9-6.

	island_start_time	island_end_time	count_of_events
1	2019-01-31 23:59:50.000	2019-02-01 00:00:15.000	5
2	2019-02-01 00:15:00.000	2019-02-01 00:15:00.000	1
3	2019-02-01 00:30:00.000	2019-02-01 00:30:00.000	1
4	2019-02-01 00:45:00.000	2019-02-01 00:45:00.000	1
5	2019-02-01 01:00:00.000	2019-02-01 01:00:00.000	1
6	2019-02-01 01:15:00.000	2019-02-01 01:15:00.000	1
7	2019-02-01 01:30:00.000	2019-02-01 01:30:00.000	1
8	2019-02-05 03:05:00.000	2019-02-05 03:05:00.000	1
9	2019-02-12 03:05:00.000	2019-02-12 03:05:00.000	1
10	2019-02-19 03:05:00.000	2019-02-19 03:05:00.000	1
11	2019-02-20 00:00:15.000	2019-02-20 00:00:15.000	1
12	2019-02-21 00:00:13.000	2019-02-21 00:00:13.000	1
13	2019-02-22 00:00:11.000	2019-02-22 00:00:11.000	1
14	2019-02-22 22:34:01.000	2019-02-22 22:35:00.000	9
15	2019-02-23 00:00:17.000	2019-02-23 00:00:17.000	1
16	2019-02-24 00:00:12.000	2019-02-24 00:00:12.000	1
17	2019-02-25 00:00:15.000	2019-02-25 00:00:15.000	1
18	2019-02-26 00:00:12.000	2019-02-26 00:00:12.000	1
19	2019-02-26 03:05:00.000	2019-02-26 03:07:15.000	3

Figure 9-6. *Error log data, grouped by events that occur within 5 minutes of each other*

We can see that a handful of errors have been grouped together into larger data clusters, whereas the rest are not related by proximity. Anyone reviewing this data would be able to tell when significant outages occurred and could trend metrics based on the size, length, or depth of these outages.

While our results only included times and counts, we could add details about which events occurred within each range the most, least, or details of the first event in the range (as it may often be the cause of the outage).

It is important to order data uniquely. LEAD, LAG, and ROW_NUMBER must all have an ORDER BY clause that is unique. For our example here, we included *error_log_id*, an identity column, after the time. This ensures that our data is ordered uniquely the same way every time this query is executed. If the underlying data has duplicate values and we do not apply a unique sort order, then there is a risk of inconsistent or inaccurate data along those boundaries.

The key to proximity analysis is to define a rule that can be used to order data into numbered groups. With that rule we can determine the boundaries of data clusters and join them together to produce a set of grouped results. Unlike using GROUP BY, we will not know the size of our result set until runtime. The quantity of rows returned will be data-driven and could be a single row for many related events or many rows for a set of unrelated events.

If we adjust our rule, we can change the shape of our results. If events that occurred within 15 minutes of each other were related, instead of 5 minutes, then we would get a smaller data set with higher event counts. If we adjusted the rule to be narrower, counting events occurring within 1 minute of each other as related, then our result set would contain more rows and smaller counts. Experimenting with rules is a key component of this style of analytics and will help us determine which metrics are most meaningful to a given data set. When in doubt, we could automate a process that iterates through many different rules to determine which will provide the most value.

Tracking Streaks

A data cluster can represent many types of data groupings. In sports, streaks are significant and form the basis for many statistics that are used to make constant data-driven decisions. Winning and losing are the most common patterns to be reported on, but managers also track details. In baseball, hitting streaks, consecutive outs, errors, and many other metrics can be tracked as sequences of events. These sequences manifest themselves as islands or gaps that we can report on in the same fashion that we did for error log data.

For the remainder of our examples, we will use a set of baseball data that is defined in a single wide table called *dbo.GameLog*. This table contains a row per game and includes an exhaustive amount of detail, as shown in a sample in Figure 9-7.

	GameLogID	GameDate	GameNumber	GameDayofWeek	VisitingTeamName	VisitingTeamLeague	VisitingTeamGameNumber	HomeTeamName	HomeTeamLeague	HomeTeamGameNumber	VisitingScore
1	1	2015-04-05	0	Sun	SLN	NL	1	CHN	NL	1	3
2	2	2015-04-06	0	Mon	MIN	AL	1	DET	AL	1	0
3	3	2015-04-06	0	Mon	CLE	AL	1	HOU	AL	1	0
4	4	2015-04-06	0	Mon	CHA	AL	1	KCA	AL	1	1
5	5	2015-04-06	0	Mon	TOR	AL	1	NYA	AL	1	6
6	6	2015-04-06	0	Mon	TEX	AL	1	OAK	AL	1	0
7	7	2015-04-06	0	Mon	ANA	AL	1	SEA	AL	1	1
8	8	2015-04-06	0	Mon	BAL	AL	1	TBA	AL	1	6
9	9	2015-04-06	0	Mon	SFN	NL	1	ARI	NL	1	5
10	10	2015-04-06	0	Mon	PIT	NL	1	CIN	NL	1	2

Figure 9-7. *Sample of baseball game log data*

Included are details such as the weather, line score, and the names of umpires, coaches, and managers. Much of this data is missing or incomplete for older games, and so any queries we write must be tolerant of this fact. This data includes every regular season game, as well as all-star games and post-season games, for a total of 219,832 baseball games logged from 1871 through 2018.

All abbreviations, names, codes, and ambiguous dimensions have lookup tables that can be used to validate their existence or meaning. For the sake of our work, these added dimensions will be skipped as they will not provide any additional value to our analysis of streaks.

Winning and Losing Streaks

With this new data set introduced, let's dive into the most basic of streaks: winning and losing. We will define a winning streak as an island of wins bounded by losses or ties. A streak may span multiple seasons, and by default, we will not mix regular-season games with post-season games. Losing streaks are calculated the same way: as islands of losses bounded by wins or ties. While ties are infrequent in modern times, they were very common prior to the use of outdoor lighting and domed fields.

To begin, let's consider the longest winning streak in history for a specific baseball team. The query in Listing 9-7 will take game log data and group it into consecutive segments of wins and losses, creating data clusters that we can then analyze.

Listing 9-7. TSQL that Calculates All Winning Streaks by a Team and Orders by Longest First

```
WITH GAME_LOG AS (
        SELECT
                CASE WHEN (HomeScore > VisitingScore AND
                HomeTeamName = 'NYA') OR (VisitingScore > HomeScore AND
                VisitingTeamName = 'NYA') THEN 'W'
                        WHEN (HomeScore > VisitingScore AND
                        VisitingTeamName = 'NYA') OR (VisitingScore >
                        HomeScore AND HomeTeamName = 'NYA') THEN 'L'
                        WHEN VisitingScore = HomeScore THEN 'T'
                END AS result,
                LAG(CASE WHEN (HomeScore > VisitingScore AND
                HomeTeamName = 'NYA') OR (VisitingScore > HomeScore AND
                VisitingTeamName = 'NYA') THEN 'W'
                        WHEN (HomeScore > VisitingScore AND
                        VisitingTeamName = 'NYA') OR (VisitingScore >
                        HomeScore AND HomeTeamName = 'NYA') THEN 'L'
                        WHEN VisitingScore = HomeScore THEN 'T' END) OVER
                        (ORDER BY GameLog.GameDate, GameLog.GameLogId) AS
                        previous_game_result,
                LEAD(CASE WHEN (HomeScore > VisitingScore AND
                HomeTeamName = 'NYA') OR (VisitingScore > HomeScore AND
                VisitingTeamName = 'NYA') THEN 'W'
                        WHEN (HomeScore > VisitingScore AND
                        VisitingTeamName = 'NYA') OR (VisitingScore >
                        HomeScore AND HomeTeamName = 'NYA') THEN 'L'
                        WHEN VisitingScore = HomeScore THEN 'T' END) OVER
                        (ORDER BY GameLog.GameDate, GameLog.GameLogId) AS
                        next_game_result,
                ROW_NUMBER() OVER (ORDER BY GameLog.GameDate, GameLog.
                GameLogId) AS island_location,
                GameLog.GameDate,
                GameLog.GameLogId
        FROM dbo.GameLog
```

```
        WHERE GameLog.HomeTeamName = 'NYA' OR GameLog.VisitingTeamName = 'NYA'
        AND GameLog.GameType = 'REG'),
CTE_ISLAND_START AS (
        SELECT
                ROW_NUMBER() OVER (ORDER BY GAME_LOG.GameDate, GAME_LOG.
                GameLogId) AS island_number,
                GAME_LOG.GameDate AS island_start_time,
                GAME_LOG.island_location AS island_start_location
        FROM GAME_LOG
        WHERE GAME_LOG.result = 'W'
        AND (GAME_LOG.previous_game_result <> 'W' OR GAME_LOG.previous_
        game_result IS NULL)),
CTE_ISLAND_END AS (
        SELECT
                ROW_NUMBER() OVER (ORDER BY GAME_LOG.GameDate, GAME_LOG.
                GameLogId) AS island_number,
                GAME_LOG.GameDate AS island_end_time,
                GAME_LOG.island_location AS island_end_location
        FROM GAME_LOG
        WHERE GAME_LOG.result = 'W'
        AND (GAME_LOG.next_game_result <> 'W' OR GAME_LOG.next_game_result
        IS NULL))
SELECT
        CTE_ISLAND_START.island_start_time,
        CTE_ISLAND_END.island_end_time,
        CTE_ISLAND_END.island_end_location - CTE_ISLAND_START.island_start_
        location + 1 AS count_of_events,
        DATEDIFF(DAY, CTE_ISLAND_START.island_start_time, CTE_ISLAND_END.
        island_end_time) + 1 AS length_of_streak_in_days
FROM CTE_ISLAND_START
INNER JOIN CTE_ISLAND_END
ON CTE_ISLAND_START.island_number = CTE_ISLAND_END.island_number
ORDER BY CTE_ISLAND_END.island_end_location - CTE_ISLAND_START.island_
start_location DESC;
```

For this example, we are looking for the longest winning streak for the New York Yankees (NYA). We have intentionally retained the structure of our islands query from earlier in this chapter. By reusing this code, our work will be greatly simplified as the questions we ask become more challenging. Our first CTE filters our data to only include games that the Yankees played in. It also illustrates that LAG and LEAD can be used to provide more complex metrics, in this case the result of a previous game using a CASE statement.

The second and third CTEs are very similar and define the start and end of each winning streak via the use of a filter that determines the boundary between winning streak and ties/losses. Note that we check for NULL in both cases to ensure that we account for the first and last rows in our data set, which will have no events before or after them.

The final SELECT statement is almost identical to the one we implemented earlier. The only addition is a DATEDIFF to determine the length in days of the winning streak. We order by streak length so that the longest appear at the top of the list. Excluding post-season games and ties, the results in Figure 9-8 provide the output of this query.

	island_start_time	island_end_time	count_of_events	length_of_streak_in_days
1	1947-06-29	1947-07-17	19	19
2	1953-05-27	1953-06-14	18	19
3	1960-09-16	1960-10-08	16	23
4	1926-05-10	1926-05-26	16	17
5	1941-06-28	1941-07-13	14	16
6	1954-07-03	1954-07-18	13	16
7	1961-09-01	1961-09-12	13	12
8	1939-05-09	1939-05-23	12	15
9	1905-07-23	1905-08-07	12	16
10	1926-07-21	1926-08-01	11	12

Figure 9-8. *Yankees winning streaks, with the longest at the top of the list*

We can see that the longest winning streak occurred from June 29 through July 17 in 1947 and spanned 19 games over the course of 18 days. If we replace W with L in *CTE_ISLAND_START* and *CTE_ISLAND_END*, we can return the longest losing streaks for the Yankees, as seen in Figure 9-9.

	island_start_time	island_end_time	count_of_events	length_of_streak_in_days
1	1908-07-23	1908-08-06	12	15
2	1913-05-26	1913-06-06	11	12
3	1911-10-03	1912-04-20	11	201
4	1916-07-29	1916-08-05	9	8
5	1945-08-11	1945-08-18	9	8
6	1972-10-01	1973-04-09	9	191
7	1953-06-21	1953-07-01	9	11
8	1982-09-13	1982-09-21	9	9
9	1912-09-12	1912-09-21	9	10
10	1912-09-24	1912-10-04	9	11

Figure 9-9. *Yankees losing streaks, with the longest at the top of the list*

Streaks Across Partitioned Data Sets

While determining a winning or losing streak for a single team vs. all opponents is useful, we might want to know the performance of a team vs. each other team individually. This introduces a new challenge: the need to partition data as we apply gaps/islands analysis to return results for each opposing team.

This could easily be accomplished by creating a list of teams and iterating through them one by one. This would be a slow approach that would lack the creativity that our process so far has afforded us. An alternative to this would be to adjust how we use window functions to not only order by date and ID but also partition by the opposing team.

Let's consider the winning streaks for the Boston Red Sox vs. each other team in Major League Baseball. To calculate the longest winning streaks against any individual team, we will need to make the following adjustments to our code:

1. Partition all window functions by the opposing team.

2. Add the opposing team to the GAME_LOG common table expression.

3. When selecting our final data set, join on opposing team in addition to the island number.

Listing 9-8 illustrates our modified query that will return streaks vs. any given opposing team.

Listing 9-8. TSQL That Calculates All Winning Streaks by a Team vs. Each Opposing Team

```
WITH GAME_LOG AS (
        SELECT
                CASE WHEN (HomeScore > VisitingScore AND
                HomeTeamName = 'BOS') OR (VisitingScore > HomeScore AND
                VisitingTeamName = 'BOS') THEN 'W'
                        WHEN (HomeScore > VisitingScore AND
                        VisitingTeamName = 'BOS') OR (VisitingScore >
                        HomeScore AND HomeTeamName = 'BOS') THEN 'L'
                        WHEN VisitingScore = HomeScore THEN 'T'
                END AS result,
                LAG(CASE WHEN (HomeScore > VisitingScore AND
                HomeTeamName = 'BOS') OR (VisitingScore > HomeScore AND
                VisitingTeamName = 'BOS') THEN 'W'
                        WHEN (HomeScore > VisitingScore AND
                        VisitingTeamName = 'BOS') OR (VisitingScore >
                        HomeScore AND HomeTeamName = 'BOS') THEN 'L'
                        WHEN VisitingScore = HomeScore THEN 'T' END) OVER
                        (PARTITION BY CASE WHEN VisitingTeamName = 'BOS'
                        THEN HomeTeamName ELSE VisitingTeamName END
                                ORDER BY GameLog.GameDate, GameLog.
                                GameLogId) AS previous_game_result,
                LEAD(CASE WHEN (HomeScore > VisitingScore AND
                HomeTeamName = 'BOS') OR (VisitingScore > HomeScore AND
                VisitingTeamName = 'BOS') THEN 'W'
                        WHEN (HomeScore > VisitingScore AND
                        VisitingTeamName = 'BOS') OR (VisitingScore >
                        HomeScore AND HomeTeamName = 'BOS') THEN 'L'
                        WHEN VisitingScore = HomeScore THEN 'T' END) OVER
                        (PARTITION BY CASE WHEN VisitingTeamName = 'BOS'
                        THEN HomeTeamName ELSE VisitingTeamName END
                                ORDER BY GameLog.GameDate, GameLog.
                                GameLogId) AS next_game_result,
```

159

```
                ROW_NUMBER() OVER (PARTITION BY CASE WHEN VisitingTeamName
                = 'BOS' THEN HomeTeamName ELSE VisitingTeamName END ORDER
                BY GameLog.GameDate, GameLog.GameLogId) AS island_location,
                CASE WHEN VisitingTeamName = 'BOS' THEN HomeTeamName ELSE
                VisitingTeamName END AS opposing_team,
                GameLog.GameDate,
                GameLog.GameLogId
        FROM dbo.GameLog
        WHERE GameLog.GameType = 'REG'
        AND GameLog.HomeTeamName = 'BOS' OR GameLog.VisitingTeamName = 'BOS'),
CTE_ISLAND_START AS (
        SELECT
                ROW_NUMBER() OVER (PARTITION BY GAME_LOG.opposing_team
                ORDER BY GAME_LOG.GameDate, GAME_LOG.GameLogId) AS island_
                number,
                GAME_LOG.GameDate AS island_start_time,
                GAME_LOG.island_location AS island_start_location,
                GAME_LOG.opposing_team
        FROM GAME_LOG
        WHERE GAME_LOG.result = 'W'
        AND (GAME_LOG.previous_game_result <> 'W' OR GAME_LOG.previous_
        game_result IS NULL)),
CTE_ISLAND_END AS (
        SELECT
                ROW_NUMBER() OVER (PARTITION BY GAME_LOG.opposing_team
                ORDER BY GAME_LOG.GameDate, GAME_LOG.GameLogId) AS island_
                number,
                GAME_LOG.GameDate AS island_end_time,
                GAME_LOG.island_location AS island_end_location,
                GAME_LOG.opposing_team
        FROM GAME_LOG
        WHERE GAME_LOG.result = 'W'
        AND (GAME_LOG.next_game_result <> 'W' OR GAME_LOG.next_game_result
        IS NULL))
```

```
SELECT
       CTE_ISLAND_START.island_start_time,
       CTE_ISLAND_START.opposing_team,
       CTE_ISLAND_END.island_end_time,
       CTE_ISLAND_END.island_end_location - CTE_ISLAND_START.island_start_
       location + 1 AS count_of_events,
       DATEDIFF(DAY, CTE_ISLAND_START.island_start_time, CTE_ISLAND_END.
       island_end_time) + 1 AS length_of_streak_in_days
FROM CTE_ISLAND_START
INNER JOIN CTE_ISLAND_END
ON CTE_ISLAND_START.island_number = CTE_ISLAND_END.island_number
AND CTE_ISLAND_START.opposing_team = CTE_ISLAND_END.opposing_team
ORDER BY CTE_ISLAND_END.island_end_location - CTE_ISLAND_START.island_
start_location DESC;
```

Partitioning our data further adds complexity to our initial common table expression, but our subsequent code is quite similar to what we have previously written. Figure 9-10 shows this partitioned data set and how the results differ from our previous streak calculations.

	island_start_time	opposing_team	island_end_time	count_of_events	length_of_streak_in_days
1	1903-08-31	WS1	1904-09-06	22	373
2	1940-07-02	PHA	1941-05-27	18	330
3	1911-10-03	NYA	1912-07-01	17	273
4	1977-05-04	SEA	1978-06-17	15	410
5	1949-07-06	WS1	1949-09-27	14	84
6	2005-09-03	BAL	2006-05-16	13	256
7	1936-09-27	PHA	1937-08-17	13	325
8	1921-08-05	CHA	1922-05-15	12	284
9	1950-06-23	SLA	1950-08-24	12	63
10	1950-04-23	PHA	1950-08-17	12	117

Figure 9-10. *Red Sox winning streaks vs. each opposing team*

We can see that the Red Sox had a streak of 22 wins in a row vs. the Washington Senators, a feat that spanned over a year! By partitioning the data set by opposing team, we are no longer analyzing all games as a set, but games against each other team as a set of sets.

This technique can be used to isolate patterns within a set of data and understand how performance varies against different challenges. Sometimes a winning streak is separated by so much other data and by so much time that it may not be readily apparent without isolating it from that noise.

We can take these analytics a step further to calculate all winning streaks of all teams vs. all other teams in a single query. This removes the need to hard-code team names and will get us quite a bit of additional data, assuming we want to collect it simultaneously for all teams. Listing 9-9 shows how we can accomplish this. More TSQL is required, but none of it is more complex than what we have already demonstrated thus far.

Listing 9-9. Query That Calculates Winning Streaks for All Teams vs. All Other Teams

```
WITH GAME_LOG AS (
        SELECT
                CASE WHEN HomeScore > VisitingScore THEN 'W'
                        WHEN VisitingScore > HomeScore THEN 'L'
                        WHEN HomeScore = VisitingScore THEN 'T'
                END AS result,
                VisitingTeamName AS opposing_team,
                HomeTeamName AS team_to_trend,
                GameLog.GameDate,
                GameLog.GameLogId
        FROM dbo.GameLog
        WHERE GameLog.GameType = 'REG'
        UNION ALL
        SELECT
                CASE WHEN VisitingScore > HomeScore THEN 'W'
                        WHEN HomeScore > VisitingScore THEN 'L'
                END AS result,
                HomeTeamName AS opposing_team,
                VisitingTeamName AS team_to_trend,
                GameLog.GameDate,
                GameLog.GameLogId
```

```
        FROM dbo.GameLog
        WHERE GameLog.GameType = 'REG'
        AND VisitingScore <> HomeScore),
GAME_LOG_ORDERED AS (
        SELECT
                GAME_LOG.GameLogId,
                GAME_LOG.GameDate,
                GAME_LOG.team_to_trend,
                GAME_LOG.opposing_team,
                GAME_LOG.result,
                LAG(GAME_LOG.result) OVER (PARTITION BY team_to_trend,
                opposing_team ORDER BY GAME_LOG.GameDate, GAME_LOG.
                GameLogId) AS previous_game_result,
                LEAD(GAME_LOG.result) OVER (PARTITION BY team_to_trend,
                opposing_team ORDER BY GAME_LOG.GameDate, GAME_LOG.
                GameLogId) AS next_game_result,
                ROW_NUMBER() OVER (PARTITION BY team_to_trend, opposing_
                team ORDER BY GAME_LOG.GameDate, GAME_LOG.GameLogId) AS
                island_location
        FROM GAME_LOG),
CTE_ISLAND_START AS (
        SELECT
                ROW_NUMBER() OVER (PARTITION BY GAME_LOG_ORDERED.team_to_
                trend, GAME_LOG_ORDERED.opposing_team ORDER BY GAME_LOG_
                ORDERED.GameDate, GAME_LOG_ORDERED.GameLogId) AS island_
                number,
                GAME_LOG_ORDERED.GameDate AS island_start_time,
                GAME_LOG_ORDERED.island_location AS island_start_location,
                GAME_LOG_ORDERED.opposing_team,
                GAME_LOG_ORDERED.team_to_trend
        FROM GAME_LOG_ORDERED
        WHERE GAME_LOG_ORDERED.result = 'W'
        AND (GAME_LOG_ORDERED.previous_game_result <> 'W' OR GAME_LOG_
        ORDERED.previous_game_result IS NULL)),
```

```
CTE_ISLAND_END AS (
       SELECT
                 ROW_NUMBER() OVER (PARTITION BY GAME_LOG_ORDERED.team_to_
                 trend, GAME_LOG_ORDERED.opposing_team ORDER BY GAME_LOG_
                 ORDERED.GameDate, GAME_LOG_ORDERED.GameLogId) AS island_
                 number,
                 GAME_LOG_ORDERED.GameDate AS island_end_time,
                 GAME_LOG_ORDERED.island_location AS island_end_location,
                 GAME_LOG_ORDERED.opposing_team,
                 GAME_LOG_ORDERED.team_to_trend
       FROM GAME_LOG_ORDERED
       WHERE GAME_LOG_ORDERED.result = 'W'
       AND (GAME_LOG_ORDERED.next_game_result <> 'W' OR GAME_LOG_ORDERED.
       next_game_result IS NULL))
SELECT
       CTE_ISLAND_START.island_start_time,
       CTE_ISLAND_START.team_to_trend,
       CTE_ISLAND_START.opposing_team,
       CTE_ISLAND_END.island_end_time,
       CTE_ISLAND_END.island_end_location - CTE_ISLAND_START.island_start_
       location + 1 AS count_of_events,
       DATEDIFF(DAY, CTE_ISLAND_START.island_start_time, CTE_ISLAND_END.
       island_end_time) + 1 AS length_of_streak_in_days
FROM CTE_ISLAND_START
INNER JOIN CTE_ISLAND_END
ON CTE_ISLAND_START.island_number = CTE_ISLAND_END.island_number
AND CTE_ISLAND_START.opposing_team = CTE_ISLAND_END.opposing_team
AND CTE_ISLAND_START.team_to_trend = CTE_ISLAND_END.team_to_trend
ORDER BY CTE_ISLAND_END.island_end_location - CTE_ISLAND_START.island_
start_location DESC;
```

To generalize our results, we need to turn game results into a one-dimensional data set where there is simply one team vs. the other team, without a distinction between home and visiting teams. To accomplish this, we use our first CTE to flatten our game data into a single set of games. We use caution to only count ties once, otherwise we might skew the results.

The second CTE takes this data and applies LAG, LEAD, and ROW_NUMBER to provide the basis for gaps/islands analysis. The remainder of our query is very similar to before, with the addition of a join to ensure that we compile our streaks based on a trending team, opposing team, and the island number. The results of this expanded analysis can be found in Figure 9-11.

	island_start_time	team_to_trend	opposing_team	island_end_time	count_of_events	length_of_streak_in_days
1	1883-06-14	PRO	DTN	1884-09-18	27	463
2	1969-05-10	BAL	KCA	1970-08-02	23	450
3	1896-06-15	CIN	SLN	1897-09-26	23	469
4	1903-08-31	BOS	WS1	1904-09-06	22	373
5	1883-05-04	BSN	PHI	1884-06-03	22	397
6	1927-05-10	NYA	SLA	1927-09-10	21	124
7	1937-05-31	PIT	CIN	1938-04-24	20	329
8	1927-07-15	SLN	PHI	1928-07-20	20	372
9	1938-08-12	NYA	PHA	1939-05-28	19	290
10	1909-06-12	CHN	BSN	1909-09-26	19	107

Figure 9-11. *Winning streaks for each team vs. all opposing teams*

We can see that the longest winning streak of any one team vs. another in history occurred from 1883 to 1884 between the Detroit Wolverines and Providence Grays. The Red Sox 22-game winning streak from earlier shows up 4th on this list.

A final task we can accomplish is to determine the longest winning streaks overall for all teams shown in Listing 9-10, rather than for a team vs. a specific other team. This will be a surprisingly similar process and will highlight how consistent coding practices can allow us to reuse quite a bit of our TSQL and reduce the chances of a mistake along the way.

Listing 9-10. Query That Calculates Overall Winning Streaks for All Teams

```
WITH GAME_LOG AS (
        SELECT
                CASE WHEN HomeScore > VisitingScore THEN 'W'
                        WHEN VisitingScore > HomeScore THEN 'L'
                        WHEN HomeScore = VisitingScore THEN 'T'
                END AS result,
                VisitingTeamName AS opposing_team,
                HomeTeamName AS team_to_trend,
```

```
                GameLog.GameDate,
                GameLog.GameLogId
        FROM dbo.GameLog
        WHERE GameLog.GameType = 'REG'
        UNION ALL
        SELECT
                CASE WHEN VisitingScore > HomeScore THEN 'W'
                        WHEN HomeScore > VisitingScore THEN 'L'
                END AS result,
                HomeTeamName AS opposing_team,
                VisitingTeamName AS team_to_trend,
                GameLog.GameDate,
                GameLog.GameLogId
        FROM dbo.GameLog
        WHERE GameLog.GameType = 'REG'
        AND VisitingScore <> HomeScore),
GAME_LOG_ORDERED AS (
        SELECT
                GAME_LOG.GameLogId,
                GAME_LOG.GameDate,
                GAME_LOG.team_to_trend,
                GAME_LOG.result,
                LAG(GAME_LOG.result) OVER (PARTITION BY team_to_trend ORDER
                BY GAME_LOG.GameDate, GAME_LOG.GameLogId) AS previous_game_
                result,
                LEAD(GAME_LOG.result) OVER (PARTITION BY team_to_trend
                ORDER BY GAME_LOG.GameDate, GAME_LOG.GameLogId) AS next_
                game_result,
                ROW_NUMBER() OVER (PARTITION BY team_to_trend ORDER BY
                GAME_LOG.GameDate, GAME_LOG.GameLogId) AS island_location
        FROM GAME_LOG),
```

166

```
CTE_ISLAND_START AS (
        SELECT
                ROW_NUMBER() OVER (PARTITION BY GAME_LOG_ORDERED.team_to_
                trend ORDER BY GAME_LOG_ORDERED.GameDate, GAME_LOG_ORDERED.
                GameLogId) AS island_number,
                GAME_LOG_ORDERED.GameDate AS island_start_time,
                GAME_LOG_ORDERED.island_location AS island_start_location,
                GAME_LOG_ORDERED.team_to_trend
        FROM GAME_LOG_ORDERED
        WHERE GAME_LOG_ORDERED.result = 'W'
        AND (GAME_LOG_ORDERED.previous_game_result <> 'W' OR GAME_LOG_
        ORDERED.previous_game_result IS NULL)),
CTE_ISLAND_END AS (
        SELECT
                ROW_NUMBER() OVER (PARTITION BY GAME_LOG_ORDERED.team_to_
                trend ORDER BY GAME_LOG_ORDERED.GameDate, GAME_LOG_ORDERED.
                GameLogId) AS island_number,
                GAME_LOG_ORDERED.GameDate AS island_end_time,
                GAME_LOG_ORDERED.island_location AS island_end_location,
                GAME_LOG_ORDERED.team_to_trend
        FROM GAME_LOG_ORDERED
        WHERE GAME_LOG_ORDERED.result = 'W'
        AND (GAME_LOG_ORDERED.next_game_result <> 'W' OR GAME_LOG_ORDERED.
        next_game_result IS NULL))
SELECT
        CTE_ISLAND_START.island_start_time,
        CTE_ISLAND_START.team_to_trend,
        CTE_ISLAND_END.island_end_time,
        CTE_ISLAND_END.island_end_location - CTE_ISLAND_START.island_start_
        location + 1 AS count_of_events,
        DATEDIFF(DAY, CTE_ISLAND_START.island_start_time, CTE_ISLAND_END.
        island_end_time) + 1 AS length_of_streak_in_days
FROM CTE_ISLAND_START
INNER JOIN CTE_ISLAND_END
ON CTE_ISLAND_START.island_number = CTE_ISLAND_END.island_number
```

AND CTE_ISLAND_START.team_to_trend = CTE_ISLAND_END.team_to_trend
ORDER BY CTE_ISLAND_END.island_end_location - CTE_ISLAND_START.island_
start_location DESC;

To calculate overall winning streaks, we removed references to *opposing_team* from joins and window functions and let SQL Server do the rest. Figure 9-12 shows the results of these changes.

	island_start_time	team_to_trend	island_end_time	count_of_events	length_of_streak_in_days
1	1875-04-19	BS1	1875-06-03	26	46
2	2017-08-24	CLE	2017-09-14	22	22
3	1880-06-02	CHN	1880-07-08	21	37
4	1935-09-04	CHN	1935-09-27	21	24
5	1884-08-07	PRO	1884-09-06	20	31
6	2002-08-13	OAK	2002-09-04	20	23
7	1884-04-20	SLU	1884-05-22	20	33
8	1872-05-07	BS1	1872-07-04	19	59
9	1947-06-29	NYA	1947-07-17	19	19
10	1885-06-01	CHN	1885-06-24	18	24

Figure 9-12. *Longest overall winning streaks in history*

We can see that the longest streak in history was by the Boston Red Stockings in 1875, with the next longest streak taking place 142 years later by the Cleveland Indians. Since we are performing an analysis vs. all other teams, the opposition team has been removed from the results.

Data Quality

When building an analysis based on gaps or islands, we need to carefully consider the quality of the underlying data prior to crunching it. Because we are partitioning and ordering a data set into distinct endpoints, a single bad data point can throw off the remaining data within the set. There are a variety of conditions that might invalidate analytics if we do not test them first and are worth briefly discussing here.

NULL

Consider our previous analysis of baseball scores. We calculated results based on comparing scores, which resulted in the assignment of "W" for a win, "L" for a loss, or "T" for a tie. What if a score had been NULL? Our equality operations would not have returned the expected results and our analysis would be broken.

Listing 9-11 provides a query that will update the score of a single game to NULL.

Listing 9-11. Setting Scores to NULL for Data Quality Testing

```
UPDATE GameLog
      SET HomeScore = null,
              VisitingScore = null
FROM GameLog
WHERE GameLogID = 209967;
```

This row corresponds to the game for Boston on July 7, 1875. Figure 9-13 shows the winning streaks for Boston before we set a row's scores to NULL and afterward.

	island_start_time	team_to_trend	island_end_time	count_of_events	length_of_streak_in_days
40	1875-04-19	BS1	1875-06-03	26	46
41	1875-06-07	BS1	1875-06-07	1	1
42	1875-06-10	BS1	1875-06-23	8	14
43	1875-06-29	BS1	1875-06-30	2	2
44	1875-07-03	BS1	1875-08-19	13	48
45	1875-08-25	BS1	1875-09-03	5	10
46	1875-09-06	BS1	1875-10-28	15	53
47	1875-10-30	BS1	1875-10-30	1	1

	island_start_time	team_to_trend	island_end_time	count_of_events	length_of_streak_in_days
40	1875-04-19	BS1	1875-06-03	26	46
41	1875-06-07	BS1	1875-06-07	1	1
42	1875-06-10	BS1	1875-06-23	8	14
43	1875-06-29	BS1	1875-06-30	2	2
44	1875-07-03	BS1	1875-07-05	2	3
45	1875-07-08	BS1	1875-08-19	10	43
46	1875-08-25	BS1	1875-09-03	5	10
47	1875-09-06	BS1	1875-10-28	15	53
48	1875-10-30	BS1	1875-10-30	1	1

Figure 9-13. *Winning streaks for the Boston Red Stockings, before and after NULL update*

169

The presence of NULL resulted in a new island of data being created via a winning streak being broken into two. This was a fairly benign result that resulted in bad data in one location but did not destroy our entire data set. Had a more fundamental metric contained NULL, such as *GameType*, we may have seen more widespread nonsense in the results.

Unexpected or Invalid Values

As is common to any data analysis, we will often find garbage data that can throw off our work. Date fields often contain "1/1/1900" as a dummy value, strings can contain blanks, and what should be a positive integer might happen to contain -1. While we can try to validate and correct bad data when we encounter it, we should write queries that guard against it the best they can so that our analytics are not broken by a single odd entry. Here are a few suggestions for managing these scenarios:

- When using a CASE statement, either have a catch-all ELSE clause or encompass all possible options within the set of WHEN clauses.

- Consider filtering out bad data prior to analysis. This eliminates the need to code around it and its presence can be communicated to the appropriate parties at a later time.

- If bad data can be created and passed into your system, document the report such that its consumer knows its existence and limitations.

- If tolerable, fix bad data. For example, if we know that any NULL or value less than zero should be zero, then we may fix it prior to analysis, thus eliminating the problem.

Duplicate Data

Duplicates are managed in our analytics via our window functions. The key to duplicate data being correctly processed is to ensure that the ORDER BY within each window function results in a unique order.

This requires a primary or alternate key that can be relied on throughout our queries. For example, our *error_log* data from earlier in this chapter used a unique integer primary key in all ORDER BY clauses in addition to the error time. This ensured that our data was sorted by datetime first, but ordered further by the primary key, in the event that two errors occurred at the same time.

In our baseball data, we used the integer primary key in the log table to ensure a unique ordering in all queries. If a unique column doesn't exist, then consider a combination of columns that would form an alternate key and could be used to order our data effectively.

A data set must have a unique column or set of columns to accurately perform gaps/islands analytics.

If no unique column or combination of columns exists, then we have a fundamental problem with our data that will potentially invalidate our gaps/islands analysis. If this analysis is necessary, then the best solution would be to add a new unique column, such as an identity, to ensure that we can uniquely tag each row as we analyze a data set.

A data set without a primary key is challenging to analyze in general, but for many types of analytics (such as gaps/islands), our ability to accurately return results consistently cannot be guaranteed without it.

Performance

Window functions provide the ability to produce unique metrics that would be challenging to return otherwise in T-SQL. Like all analytical processes, performance will be based on the amount of data that needs to be scanned prior to analysis. Calculating winning streaks for a single team across 10k rows of data will require scanning 10k rows. Doing so for a data set of a billion rows would require reading all billion rows. We can manage and improve performance by reconsidering the data set itself and how we access it.

The following are some options that can help facilitate better performance when performing gaps/islands analysis on a large data set, in the event that performance is not adequate:

1. Target an OLAP/reporting database. Any large-scale analytics will cause contention when run against a database with a highly transactional workload. Consider a reporting environment supported by replication, AlwaysOn, ETL, log shipping, or some other data copy process that separates analytical workloads from transactional ones.

2. If these queries must be run against an OLTP environment, run them off-hours or at a time when there are fewer other processes running.

3. The underlying filters at the beginning of each query reduce the size of the data to be analyzed. Indexing the column(s) in those filters will ensure that you do not read any additional data that is not required to satisfy the query. This allows data to be sliced into narrower sets that can be individually analyzed independently from the rest of the data set.

4. Incremental data loads can greatly help reduce the data needed to satisfy analytics that are requested regularly. If gaps/islands are crunched daily, then one only needs to recalculate metrics for the previous day to get results. The only caveat is to start the analysis from the end of the last known gap or island. This ensures that an event-in-progress at the start of the reporting period is fully reported as a single event, and as not two events split by the end of one data load and the start of the next.

5. Automate analytics so that these tasks are performed unattended and the results stored in a table for future inspection. If the results of a gaps/islands analysis are placed into a permanent repository, then future reporting requires only reading that table rather than executing complex queries each time they are required.

Summary

Window functions such as LEAD, LAG, and ROW_NUMBER can be combined to allow for a wide variety of analytics to be performed against a data set. In this chapter we demonstrated their use in finding missing data, in aggregating related events, and in calculating different types of streaks.

There are many other metrics that we can collect using methods similar to this. Gaps and islands analysis can be used to order data and determine how rows relate to those nearby in the overall set. They can allow us to locate anomalies that otherwise might not be apparent within a large/complex set of tables.

Calculating streaks allows us to string together significant chains of events over time, but we can also consider droughts. How long does time pass in between significant events, and does the probability of events occurring increase after an extended drought? Any gaps analysis can also be used to produce islands and conversely, islands analysis can be used to generate gaps data. In this regard, we can always consider both the presence of important events and the absence of those events as metrics worthy of consideration.

Once we structure queries that can perform these analytics, we can reuse our code with minimal change to process other data sets, change filters, or crunch the data in completely different ways. By experimenting with filters and the contents of the window functions we use, the potential applications for these analytics are limitless!

CHAPTER 10

Time Range Calculations

A very common reporting requirement is to produce totals by different ranges of time for comparison. Typical reports will contain totals by month, quarter, and year, sometimes with comparisons to the same period in the prior year or for month-to-date or year-to-date totals. Products like SQL Server Analysis Services and Power BI provide functions to navigate date hierarchies. With window functions in SQL Server 2012 or later, you can produce the same calculations using the techniques provided earlier in this book.

In this chapter you will put all the techniques you have learned previously to work to create calculations for navigating the timeline to produce the following calculations:

- Percent of Parent

- Year-to-date (YTD)

- Quarter-to-date (QTD)

- Month-to-date (MTD)

- Same Period Prior Year (SP PY)

- Prior year-to-date (PY YTD)

- Average, moving average (MA)

- Growth, growth percentage

You have learned about using window aggregates to add summaries to queries without grouping in Chapter 3, accumulating aggregates in Chapter 4, and frames in Chapter 5. You will be putting these all together, with a bit of common sense to create complex calculations that without the use of window functions would have required a lot more steps.

© Kathi Kellenberger, Clayton Groom, and Ed Pollack 2019
K. Kellenberger et al., *Expert T-SQL Window Functions in SQL Server 2019*,
https://doi.org/10.1007/978-1-4842-5197-3_10

Remember, in the case of accumulating aggregates, the PARTITION BY and ORDER BY determine which rows end up in the window. The FRAME DEFINITION is used to define the subset of rows from within the partition that will be aggregated. The examples in this section use the frame definition to do the heavy lifting. To review, here's the syntax:

```
<AggregateFunction>(<col1>) OVER([PARTITION BY <col2>[,<col3>,...<colN>]]
    ORDER BY <col4>[,<col5>,...<colN>] [Frame definition])
```

In this chapter, you will need to use the AdventureWorksDW sample database.

Percent of Parent

Comparing the performance of a product in a specific period to the performance for all products in that same period, or each product in a category to the category, is a very common analytic technique. In this next set of examples, you will build upon the simple base query in Listing 10-1, by adding columns that calculate the pieces needed to produce the final "Percent of Parent" results as shown in Figure 10-1. You will start out with a straightforward query that aggregates sales by month and will add new calculation columns as they are covered, enabling each new column to be introduced on its own without needing to replicate the entire block of example code for each iteration.

Listing 10-1. Base Query

```
--10.1 Base query. Just your average GROUP BY.
SELECT f.ProductKey,
    YEAR(f.orderdate) AS OrderYear,
    MONTH(f.orderdate) AS OrderMonth,
    SUM(f.SalesAmount) AS [Sales]
FROM dbo.FactInternetSales AS f
WHERE OrderDate BETWEEN '2011-01-01' AND '2012-12-31'
GROUP BY f.ProductKey,
    YEAR(f.orderdate),
    MONTH(f.orderdate)
ORDER BY 2, 3, f.ProductKey;
```

	ProductKey	OrderYear	OrderMonth	Sales
1	310	2011	1	78721.94
2	311	2011	1	78721.94
3	312	2011	1	96613.29
4	313	2011	1	53674.05
5	314	2011	1	60830.59
6	322	2011	1	699.0982

Figure 10-1. *Results of our simple base query*

"Percent of Parent" or "Ratio to Parent" calculations can be generally defined as "[Child Total] / [Parent Total]". In order to calculate the ratio as defined, you need to calculate the numerator and denominator inputs and combine them in a third measure. To calculate the overall contribution each product has made to all sales, you need to determine the total for [All Sales] and for [Product All Sales]. Once you have those defined, you can calculate [Ratio to All Sales] as [Product All Sales] / [All Sales]. You can multiply the resulting ratio by 100 to display it as a percentage or rely on the formatting functions in the reporting or front-end tool to display them as percentages.

For each of these measures, the window aggregate SUM() function encapsulates a regular SUM() function, which might look a little bit strange to begin with, but is required to aggregate [SalesAmount] to levels higher than the level of granularity of the query. The result, as shown in Figure 10-2, is the ability to aggregate the same source column to different levels in a single query without having to resort to temporary tables or common table expressions.

The code in Listing 10-2 contains the additional column logic you need to append to the base query, just after the last column in the select list. Be sure to include a comma after [Sales].

Listing 10-2. Additional Columns for [All Sales]

```
SUM(SUM(f.SalesAmount)) OVER () AS [All Sales],
SUM(SUM(f.SalesAmount)) OVER (PARTITION BY f.productkey)
    AS [Product All Sales],
SUM(SUM(f.SalesAmount)) OVER (PARTITION BY f.productkey)
    / SUM(SUM(f.SalesAmount)) OVER()
    AS [Ratio to All Sales]
```

	ProductKey	OrderYear	OrderMonth	Sales	All Sales	Product All Sales	Ratio to All Sales
1	310	2011	1	78721.94	12918011.1243	1195142.18	0.0925
2	311	2011	1	78721.94	12918011.1243	1001915.60	0.0775
3	312	2011	1	96613.29	12918011.1243	1198720.45	0.0927
4	313	2011	1	53674.05	12918011.1243	1077059.27	0.0833
5	314	2011	1	60830.59	12918011.1243	1052011.38	0.0814
6	322	2011	1	699.0982	12918011.1243	11884.6694	0.0009
7	324	2011	1	699.0982	12918011.1243	11185.5712	0.0008
8	326	2011	1	1398.1964	12918011.1243	15380.1604	0.0011
9	328	2011	1	699.0982	12918011.1243	18176.5532	0.0014

Figure 10-2. *Results of calculating product sales as a percentage of all sales*

The frame for the [All Sales] column does not have a PARTITION clause, which means it will aggregate across all the data available to the query, providing a total of sales for all time. This value will be the same for each row in the resulting table. The PARTITION clause for the [Product All Sales] column restricts the partition to each instance of a product key, providing a total of sales by product for all time. This value will be the same for all rows sharing the same [ProductKey] value.

The [Ratio to All Sales] column combines the two prior statements to calculate the ratio between them. The key thing to realize is that you can combine the results of multiple aggregation results within a single column. Knowing this will allow you to create all manner of complex calculations that otherwise would have been relegated to a reporting tool or application code. Writing the calculations out in simple terms is a good way to document what you want to accomplish and provides a template for combining existing calculations together to form new ones. The following pseudo-code maps out the logic that will be implemented in T-SQL:

```
[Sales] = SUM of SalesAmount by Product, Year and Month
[All Sales] = SUM of SalesAmount for all Products and all dates
[Annual Sales] = SUM of SalesAmount for all Products, by Year
[Month All Sales] = SUM of SalesAmount for all Product by Year and Month
[Product All Sales] = SUM of SalesAmount by Product, for all dates
[Product Annual Sales] = SUM of SalesAmount by Product, by Year
[Ratio to All Sales] = [Product All Sales] / [All Sales]
[Ratio to Annual Sales] = [Product Annual Sales] / [Annual Sales]
[Ratio to Month Sales] = [Sales] / [Month All Sales]
```

This approach works best if you work out the logic for each input column for a given calculation and then create the complex calculation that leverages the input column calculations. The column calculations for the annual and monthly levels follow a similar pattern, so once you have calculations for one level worked out, the rest will follow quickly. Later in the chapter you will learn how to use common table expressions to make the creation of complex calculations less daunting.

There is no need to worry about handling a divide-by-zero error at the "all" level, as the only case that will result in an error is if there are no rows at all in the source table, but for every level below it, you must account for situations where the denominator value can be zero. The calculations for the "annual" and "month" levels in Listing 10-3 demonstrate how this can be done. By wrapping the window SUM() statement in a NULLIF() function, any zero aggregate values is turned into a NULL value, avoiding the divide by zero error. You could also use a CASE statement instead of NULLIF(), but given the nesting of functions involved, NULLIF() is more concise.

Listing 10-3. Additional Columns to Calculate the Annual and Monthly Percentage of Parent Columns

```
--10.3 Annual and monthly Percentage of Parent
SUM(SUM(f.SalesAmount))
      OVER (PARTITION BY YEAR(f.OrderDate)) AS [Annual Sales],
   SUM(SUM(f.SalesAmount))
      OVER (PARTITION BY f.productkey, YEAR(f.OrderDate))
      AS [Product Annual Sales],
--Pct of group:
--[Ratio to Annual Sales] = [Product Annual Sales] / [Annual Sales]
   SUM(SUM(f.SalesAmount))
      OVER (PARTITION BY f.productkey, YEAR(f.OrderDate))
      / NULLIF(SUM(SUM(f.SalesAmount))
               OVER (PARTITION BY YEAR(f.OrderDate))
             , 0) AS [Ratio to Annual Sales],
   SUM(SUM(f.SalesAmount))
      OVER (PARTITION BY YEAR(f.OrderDate), MONTH(f.OrderDate))
      AS [Month All Sales],
```

```
SUM(SUM(f.SalesAmount))
    OVER (PARTITION BY f.productkey, YEAR(f.OrderDate),
            MONTH(f.OrderDate))
    / NULLIF(SUM(SUM(f.SalesAmount))
            OVER (PARTITION BY YEAR(f.OrderDate), MONTH(f.OrderDate))
            , 0) AS [Ratio to Month Sales]
```

If you want to make your code easier to read, understand, and maintain, you can calculate all of the base aggregations in one pass in a common table expression (CTE), as in Listing 10-4, and then perform the second-order calculation in a following query. Using the named result columns from the CTE instead of the expanded logic columns used earlier improves code readability dramatically. Once you have worked out the logic for any given combined calculation, you can comment out or remove the input columns and just return the final result columns that you are interested in, as shown in Figure 10-3.

Listing 10-4. Base Query with Percent of Parent Calculations for [SalesAmount]

```
--10.4 Percent of Parent, Annual and Monthly sales
--Refactored to use a CTE, making the final SELECT readable by mere mortals.

WITH CTE_Base
AS ( SELECT f.ProductKey,
        YEAR(f.orderdate) AS OrderYear,
        MONTH(f.orderdate) AS OrderMonth,
        SUM(f.SalesAmount) AS [Sales],
        SUM(SUM(f.SalesAmount)) OVER () AS [All Sales],
        SUM(SUM(f.SalesAmount)) OVER (PARTITION BY f.productkey)
            AS [Product All Sales],
        SUM(SUM(f.SalesAmount))
            OVER (PARTITION BY YEAR(f.OrderDate)) AS [Annual Sales],
        SUM(SUM(f.SalesAmount))
            OVER (PARTITION BY YEAR(f.OrderDate), MONTH(f.OrderDate))
            AS [Month All Sales],
        SUM(SUM(f.SalesAmount))
            OVER (PARTITION BY f.productkey, YEAR(f.OrderDate))
            AS [Product Annual Sales]
    FROM dbo.FactInternetSales AS f
```

```
WHERE OrderDate BETWEEN '2011-01-01' AND '2012-12-31'
GROUP BY f.ProductKey,
        YEAR(f.orderdate),
        MONTH(f.orderdate)
        )
SELECT ProductKey,
        OrderYear,
        OrderMonth,
        [Sales],
        [Product All Sales] / [All Sales] AS [Ratio to All Sales],
        [Product Annual Sales] / NULLIF([Annual Sales], 0)
                AS [Ratio to Annual Sales],
        [Sales] / NULLIF([Month All Sales], 0) AS [Ratio to Month Sales]
FROM CTE_Base
ORDER BY OrderYear,
            OrderMonth,
            ProductKey;
```

	ProductKey	OrderYear	OrderMonth	Sales	Ratio to All Sales	Ratio to Annual Sales	Ratio to Month Sales
1	310	2011	1	78721.94	0.0925	0.1689	0.1675
2	311	2011	1	78721.94	0.0775	0.1416	0.1675
3	312	2011	1	96613.29	0.0927	0.1694	0.2056
4	313	2011	1	53674.05	0.0833	0.1522	0.1142
5	314	2011	1	60830.59	0.0814	0.1486	0.1294
6	322	2011	1	699.0982	0.0009	0.0016	0.0014
7	324	2011	1	699.0982	0.0008	0.0015	0.0014
8	326	2011	1	1398.1964	0.0011	0.0021	0.0029

Figure 10-3. *The results for Listing 10-4*

Period-to-Date Calculations

Period-to-date calculations are a mainstay of financial reports but are notoriously difficult to incorporate into query-based reports without resorting to multiple CTEs or temporary tables. Typically, the grouping is performed in a reporting tool such as SQL Server Reporting Services or Excel to provide the aggregated results, but can still be tricky to implement. The examples you will work through next will show you how to create multiple levels of rolling totals in a single result set, by adding a FRAME clause after the ORDER BY clause. The frame clause is covered in more detail in Chapter 5.

Listing 10-5 demonstrates how to use the frame definition to calculate period-to-date totals by date, by product for months, quarters, and years. The base query is essentially the same as before, but the level of granularity is at the date level instead of the month level. This is so that you can see the results of the aggregate columns in more detail.

Listing 10-5. Calculating Period-to-Date Running Totals by Date

```
--10.5 day level aggregates, with rolling totals for MTD, QTD, YTD
SELECT f.OrderDate,
       f.ProductKey,
       YEAR(f.orderdate) AS OrderYear,
       MONTH(f.orderdate) AS OrderMonth,
       SUM(f.SalesAmount) AS [Sales],
       SUM(SUM(f.SalesAmount))
          OVER(PARTITION BY f.productkey, YEAR(f.orderdate),
               MONTH(f.orderdate)
               ORDER BY f.productkey, f.orderdate
               ROWS BETWEEN UNBOUNDED PRECEDING AND CURRENT ROW
             ) AS [Sales MTD],
       SUM(SUM(f.SalesAmount))
       OVER(PARTITION BY f.productkey, YEAR(f.orderdate),
            DATEPART(QUARTER, f.OrderDate)
            ORDER BY f.productkey, YEAR(f.orderdate), MONTH(f.orderdate)
            ROWS BETWEEN UNBOUNDED PRECEDING AND CURRENT ROW
          ) AS [Sales QTD],
       SUM(SUM(f.SalesAmount))
          OVER(PARTITION BY f.productkey, YEAR(f.orderdate)
          ORDER BY f.productkey, f.orderdate
          ROWS BETWEEN UNBOUNDED PRECEDING AND CURRENT ROW
        ) AS [Sales YTD],
       SUM(SUM(f.SalesAmount))
          OVER(PARTITION BY f.productkey
          ORDER BY f.productkey, f.orderdate
          ROWS BETWEEN UNBOUNDED PRECEDING AND CURRENT ROW
        ) AS [Sales Running Total]
```

```
FROM dbo.FactInternetSales AS f
GROUP BY f.orderdate, f.ProductKey, YEAR(f.orderdate), MONTH(f.orderdate)
ORDER BY f.ProductKey, f.OrderDate;
```

The OVER clause examples shown in Listing 10-5 uses the ROWS BETWEEN UNBOUNDED PRECEDING AND CURRENT ROW frame. This results in the calculation aggregating all rows from the beginning of the frame to the current row, giving you the correct total to-date for the level specified in the PARTITION clause. For instance, the [Sale Amt MTD] aggregate column will calculate the SUM([SalesAmount]) from the first day of the month, the first unbounded preceding row, through to the current row. The ORDER BY clause becomes mandatory when using a FRAME clause, providing the context for the frame to move sequentially through the rows in the PARTITION.

Figure 10-4 shows the partial results. The [Sales MTD], [Sales QTD] and [Sales YTD] column values increase until reaching a different [ProductKey] or [ProductKey] and time level (Month & Quarter). The results in Figure 10-4 show the break in aggregations at the end of the second quarter, so you can see by looking at the rows where [ProductKey] is equal to 311, 312, or 313 that the MTD and QTD aggregations reset on October 1.

	OrderDate	ProductKey	OrderYear	OrderMonth	Sales	Sales MTD	Sales QTD	Sales YTD
1163	2011-09-29 ...	311	2011	9	3578.27	100191.56	239744.09	737123.62
1164	2011-09-29 ...	312	2011	9	3578.27	110926.37	329200.84	869519.61
1165	2011-09-29 ...	313	2011	9	3578.27	75143.67	289839.87	758593.24
1166	2011-09-29 ...	328	2011	9	699.0982	699.0982	5592.7856	11884.6...
1167	2011-09-29 ...	340	2011	9	699.0982	2796.3928	6291.8838	7690.0802
1168	2011-09-30 ...	311	2011	9	3578.27	103769.83	243322.36	740701.89
1169	2011-09-30 ...	312	2011	9	3578.27	114504.64	332779.11	873097.88
1170	2011-09-30 ...	346	2011	9	3399.99	23799.93	37399.89	112199.67
1171	2011-10-01 ...	310	2011	10	7156.54	7156.54	7156.54	898145.77
1172	2011-10-01 ...	312	2011	10	7156.54	7156.54	7156.54	880254.42
1173	2011-10-01 ...	313	2011	10	3578.27	3578.27	3578.27	762171.51
1174	2011-10-01 ...	314	2011	10	7156.54	7156.54	7156.54	769328.05
1175	2011-10-01 ...	330	2011	10	699.0982	699.0982	699.0982	9787.3748
1176	2011-10-01 ...	351	2011	10	3374.99	3374.99	3374.99	111374.67
1177	2011-10-02 ...	311	2011	10	7156.54	7156.54	7156.54	747858.43
1178	2011-10-02 ...	312	2011	10	3578.27	10734.81	10734.81	883832.69
1179	2011-10-02 ...	313	2011	10	7156.54	10734.81	10734.81	769328.05

Figure 10-4. *The partial results of Listing 10-5 at the end of a quarter (September 30)*

Averages and Moving Averages
Handling Gaps in Date Ranges

Before moving on to more involved examples, you need to stop and consider the challenges faced when working with dates. Dates as a data type are continuous and sequential. The T-SQL functions that work with dates are written with this in mind and handle any involved date math correctly. In reality, data based on dates will not be continuous. Transaction data will have gaps where there is no data for a day, week, or possibly even a month or more.

Window functions are not date aware, so it is up to you to ensure that any aggregate calculations handle gaps in the data correctly. If you use the LEAD() and LAG() window functions over date ranges or date period ranges, you have to provide partitions in your result sets that contain continuous and complete sets of dates, months, quarters, or years as needed by your calculations. Failure to do so will result in incorrect results. The reason for this is that the LEAD() and LAG() functions operate over the result set of the query, moving the specified number of rows forward or backward in the result set, regardless of the number of days or months represented.

For example, a 3-month rolling average implemented incorrectly using window functions won't take into account cases where there is no data for a product in a given month. It will perform the frame subset over the data provided and produce an average over the prior three months, regardless of whether they are contiguous months or not. Listing 10-6 demonstrates how not accounting for gaps in a date range will result in incorrect or misleading results. In this example, the data is being aggregated to the month level by removing any grouping reference to [OrderDate]:

Listing 10-6. Incorrectly Handling Gaps Dates

```
--10.6 Handling gaps in dates, Month level: not handling gaps
SELECT ROW_NUMBER()
        OVER(ORDER BY f.ProductKey, YEAR(f.OrderDate), MONTH(f.OrderDate))
      AS [RowID],
    f.ProductKey,
    YEAR(f.OrderDate) AS OrderYear,
    MONTH(f.OrderDate) AS OrderMonth,
    ROUND(SUM(f.SalesAmount), 2) AS [Sales], -- month level
```

```
ROUND(SUM(SUM(f.SalesAmount))
    OVER(PARTITION BY f.ProductKey, YEAR(f.OrderDate)
        ORDER BY f.ProductKey, YEAR(f.OrderDate), MONTH(f.OrderDate)
        ROWS BETWEEN UNBOUNDED PRECEDING AND CURRENT ROW
        ), 2) AS [Sales YTD],
    ROUND(AVG(SUM(f.SalesAmount))
    OVER(PARTITION BY f.ProductKey
        ORDER BY f.ProductKey, YEAR(f.OrderDate), MONTH(f.OrderDate)
        ROWS BETWEEN 3 PRECEDING AND CURRENT ROW
        ),2) AS [3 Month Moving Avg]
FROM [dbo].[FactInternetSales] AS f
WHERE ProductKey = 332
AND f.OrderDate BETWEEN '2010-12-01' AND '2011-12-31'
GROUP BY f.ProductKey, YEAR(f.OrderDate), MONTH(f.OrderDate)
ORDER BY f.ProductKey ,YEAR(f.OrderDate), MONTH(f.OrderDate)
```

Notice in the results in Figure 10-5 that for the time range selected, only 9 months are represented. Calculating a moving average over the range of months that contain no data will produce incorrect results. You will learn how to address this next by filling in the gaps.

	RowID	ProductKey	OrderYear	OrderMonth	Sales	Sales YTD	3 Month Moving Avg
1	1	332	2011	1	2097.29	2097.29	2097.29
2	2	332	2011	4	1398.20	3495.49	1747.75
3	3	332	2011	5	699.10	4194.59	1398.20
4	4	332	2011	6	2796.39	6990.98	1747.75
5	5	332	2011	7	699.10	7690.08	1398.20
6	6	332	2011	8	1398.20	9088.28	1398.20
7	7	332	2011	9	699.10	9787.37	1398.20
8	8	332	2011	10	1398.20	11185.57	1048.65
9	9	332	2011	12	1398.20	12583.77	1223.42

Figure 10-5. *Incorrect calculation of a moving average*

In order to address this problem, a supplementary "Date" table needs to be used to fill in the gaps in the transaction data. This is not a new problem and has been solved in data warehouse designs by including a "Date" dimension table that contains a row for every date in a specified range of years. The AdventureWorksDW database contains a table DimDate that will be used in the following examples. If you do not have a date dimension at your disposal, you can also use a common table expression (CTE) to create a date dimension table. The use of a table of date values will result in much better performance over using a CTE. An example CTE-derived calendar dimension view is included in the code download.

In Listing 10-7, the DimDate table is cross joined with the DimProduct table to produce a set containing all products for all dates in the specified range. The resulting CTE "table" is used as the primary table in the SELECT portion of the query so that every date in the range is represented in the aggregated results for every product even if there were no transactions for that product in a given time period. You can also pick up additional attributes from the product table such as product category, color, etc., row counts, and distinct counts from the fact table. These can be used to create additional statistics. In Figure 10-6, you can see that [ProductAlternateKey] is added and takes the place of [ProductKey] in all grouping operations in order to make the results more user-friendly.

Listing 10-7. Correctly Handling Gaps in Dates

```
--10.7 month level. Now handling gaps in transaction dates
WITH CTE_ProductPeriod
AS (
    SELECT p.ProductKey, p.ProductAlternateKey as [ProductID],
        Datekey, CalendarYear,
        CalendarQuarter, MonthNumberOfYear AS CalendarMonth
    FROM DimDate AS d
    CROSS JOIN DimProduct p
    WHERE d.FullDateAlternateKey BETWEEN '2011-01-01' AND '2013-12-31'
    AND EXISTS(SELECT * FROM FactInternetSales f
            WHERE f.ProductKey = p.ProductKey
            AND f.OrderDate BETWEEN '2011-01-01' AND '2013-12-31')
   )
  SELECT      ROW_NUMBER()
        OVER(ORDER BY p.[ProductID],
                    p.CalendarYear,
                    p.CalendarMonth
             ) as [RowID],
        p.[ProductID],
        p.CalendarYear  AS OrderYear,
```

```
        p.CalendarMonth AS OrderMonth,
        ROUND(SUM(COALESCE(f.SalesAmount,0)), 2) AS [Sales],
        ROUND(SUM(SUM(f.SalesAmount))
                    OVER(PARTITION BY p.[ProductID], p.CalendarYear
                        ORDER BY P.[ProductID], p.CalendarYear, p.CalendarMonth
                        ROWS BETWEEN UNBOUNDED PRECEDING AND CURRENT ROW
                    ), 2) AS [Sales YTD],
        ROUND(SUM(SUM(COALESCE(f.SalesAmount, 0)))
                    OVER(PARTITION BY p.[ProductID]
                        ORDER BY p.[ProductID], p.CalendarYear, p.CalendarMonth
                        ROWS BETWEEN 3 PRECEDING AND CURRENT ROW
                    ) / 3, 2) AS [3 Month Moving Avg]
FROM CTE_ProductPeriod AS p
LEFT OUTER JOIN [dbo].[FactInternetSales] AS f
    ON p.ProductKey = f.ProductKey
    AND p.DateKey = f.OrderDateKey
WHERE p.ProductKey = 332
AND p.CalendarYear =  2011
GROUP BY p.[ProductID], p.CalendarYear, p.CalendarMonth
ORDER BY p.[ProductID], p.CalendarYear, p.CalendarMonth
```

	RowID	ProductID	OrderYear	OrderMonth	Sales	Sales YTD	3 Month Moving Avg
1	1	BK-R50B-58	2011	1	2097.29	2097.29	699.10
2	2	BK-R50B-58	2011	2	0.00	2097.29	699.10
3	3	BK-R50B-58	2011	3	0.00	2097.29	699.10
4	4	BK-R50B-58	2011	4	1398.20	3495.49	1165.16
5	5	BK-R50B-58	2011	5	699.10	4194.59	699.10
6	6	BK-R50B-58	2011	6	2796.39	6990.98	1631.23
7	7	BK-R50B-58	2011	7	699.10	7690.08	1864.26
8	8	BK-R50B-58	2011	8	1398.20	9088.28	1864.26
9	9	BK-R50B-58	2011	9	699.10	9787.37	1864.26
10	10	BK-R50B-58	2011	10	1398.20	11185.57	1398.20
11	11	BK-R50B-58	2011	11	0.00	11185.57	1165.16
12	12	BK-R50B-58	2011	12	1398.20	12583.77	1165.16

Figure 10-6. *Moving average, taking gaps in sales data into account*

Compare the results of the two previous queries. The [3 Month Moving Avg] column is now correct for the months where there were no sales for the product (February, March, November) and for the months immediately after the empty periods (May, June, December). The calculation in the second query did not use the AVG() function but rather divides the SUM() by three to arrive at the average. This ensures a more accurate average for the first three periods. In the following sections, you will learn how to limit calculations only to ranges that are complete when calculating moving averages.

Same Period Prior Year

Part and parcel with providing period-to-date calculations, you will need to provide comparisons to the same period in the prior year, the prior period in the same year, and quite possibly difference amounts and difference percentages. These aggregates can be calculated the same way as the items you have worked with so far: by defining the formula in simple terms, determining the input calculations at a column level, and then building the output column using the input calculations.

For this example, the [ProductKey] is dropped from the query so that the granularity of the results is at a month level. This makes it easier for you to see the effect of the new calculations in the smaller number of result rows. In order to calculate a value from a prior year, the query cannot be limited to a single year in the WHERE clause. Figure 10-7 shows that for a window function to be able to look back into a prior year, there must be more than one year available in the result set.

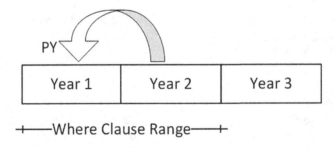

Figure 10-7. *WHERE clause has to cover dates for prior ranges*

The LAG() function can retrieve and aggregate data by looking back in the record set by the number of rows specified. It also has an optional default parameter that can be used to return a zero value for cases where there is no row available when navigating back through the records. Listing 10-8 and Figure 10-8 demonstrate this:

Listing 10-8. Retrieving Results for the Same Month of the Prior Year

```
--10.8 Same Month, Prior Year
WITH CTE_ProductPeriod
AS (
    SELECT p.ProductKey, --p.ProductAlternateKey as [ProductID],
           Datekey, CalendarYear, CalendarQuarter,
           MonthNumberOfYear AS CalendarMonth
    FROM DimDate AS d
    CROSS JOIN DimProduct p
        WHERE d.FullDateAlternateKey BETWEEN '2011-01-01' AND '2013-12-31'
        AND EXISTS(SELECT * FROM FactInternetSales f
                    WHERE f.ProductKey = p.ProductKey
                    AND f.OrderDate BETWEEN '2011-01-01' AND '2013-12-31')
    )
 SELECT
        ROW_NUMBER()
          OVER(ORDER BY p.CalendarYear, p.CalendarMonth) as [RowID],
        p.CalendarYear AS OrderYear,
        p.CalendarMonth AS OrderMonth,
        ROUND(SUM(COALESCE(f.SalesAmount,0)), 2) AS [Sales],
        ROUND(SUM(SUM(COALESCE(f.SalesAmount, 0)))
                  OVER(PARTITION BY p.CalendarYear
                      ORDER BY p.CalendarYear, p.CalendarMonth
                      ROWS BETWEEN UNBOUNDED PRECEDING AND CURRENT ROW
                      ), 2) AS [Sales YTD],
        ROUND(LAG(SUM(f.SalesAmount), 12 , 0)
              OVER(ORDER BY p.CalendarYear, p.CalendarMonth),2)
            as [Sales Same Month PY]
```

```
FROM CTE_ProductPeriod AS p
LEFT OUTER JOIN [dbo].[FactInternetSales] AS f
    ON p.ProductKey = f.ProductKey
    AND p.DateKey = f.OrderDateKey
GROUP BY p.CalendarYear, p.CalendarMonth
ORDER BY p.CalendarYear, p.CalendarMonth
```

	RowID	OrderYear	OrderMonth	Sales	Sales YTD	Sales Same Month PY
1	1	2011	1	469823.91	469823.91	0.00
2	2	2011	2	466334.90	936158.82	0.00
3	3	2011	3	485198.66	1421357.48	0.00
4	4	2011	4	502073.85	1923431.32	0.00
5	5	2011	5	561681.48	2485112.80	0.00
6	6	2011	6	737839.82	3222952.62	0.00
7	7	2011	7	596746.56	3819699.18	0.00
8	8	2011	8	614557.94	4434257.11	0.00
9	9	2011	9	603083.50	5037340.61	0.00
10	10	2011	10	708208.00	5745548.61	0.00
11	11	2011	11	660545.81	6406094.43	0.00
12	12	2011	12	669431.50	7075525.93	0.00
13	13	2012	1	495364.13	495364.13	469823.91
14	14	2012	2	506994.19	1002358.31	466334.90
15	15	2012	3	373483.01	1375841.32	485198.66

Figure 10-8. *Same month prior year*

Growth and Percent Growth

Once you can look back and pluck a value from the past, you can calculate differences between those values very easily. The commonly accepted method for calculating Percent Growth is ([current] - [previous]) / [previous]. You can also multiply the result by 100 if you want the percentage values to be in the format of "##.###". Add the following section from Listing 10-9 to the query from Listing 10-8 to incorporate the new calculations and run the query. Your results should match Figure 10-9.

Listing 10-9. Growth: Current Month Over the Same Month of the Prior Year

```
-- [Growth] = [CY] - [PY]
ROUND(SUM(COALESCE(f.SalesAmount,0))
    - LAG(SUM(f.SalesAmount), 12, 0)
        OVER(ORDER BY p.CalendarYear, p.CalendarMonth), 2)
    as [PY MOM Growth],
-- [Pct Growth] = ([CY] - [PY]) / [PY]
(SUM(COALESCE(f.SalesAmount,0))
    - LAG(SUM(f.SalesAmount), 12, 0)
        OVER(ORDER BY p.CalendarYear, p.CalendarMonth)
    ) / nullif(LAG(SUM(f.SalesAmount), 12, 0 )
        OVER(ORDER BY p.CalendarYear, p.CalendarMonth), 0)
    as [PY MOM Growth %]
```

	RowID	OrderYear	OrderMonth	Sales	Sales YTD	Sales Same Month PY	PY MOM Growth	PY MOM Growth %
1	1	2011	1	469823.91	469823.91	0.00	469823.91	NULL
2	2	2011	2	466334.90	936158.82	0.00	466334.90	NULL
3	3	2011	3	485198.66	1421357.48	0.00	485198.66	NULL
4	4	2011	4	502073.85	1923431.32	0.00	502073.85	NULL
5	5	2011	5	561681.48	2485112.80	0.00	561681.48	NULL
6	6	2011	6	737839.82	3222952.62	0.00	737839.82	NULL
7	7	2011	7	596746.56	3819699.18	0.00	596746.56	NULL
8	8	2011	8	614557.94	4434257.11	0.00	614557.94	NULL
9	9	2011	9	603083.50	5037340.61	0.00	603083.50	NULL
10	10	2011	10	708208.00	5745548.61	0.00	708208.00	NULL
11	11	2011	11	660545.81	6406094.43	0.00	660545.81	NULL
12	12	2011	12	669431.50	7075525.93	0.00	669431.50	NULL
13	13	2012	1	495364.13	495364.13	469823.91	25540.21	0.0543
14	14	2012	2	506994.19	1002358.31	466334.90	40659.28	0.0871
15	15	2012	3	373483.01	1375841.32	485198.66	-111715.65	-0.2302
16	16	2012	4	400335.61	1776176.93	502073.85	-101738.23	-0.2026

Figure 10-9. Growth: Current month over the same month of the prior year

The same approach can be used to determine the value for the prior month and the difference between it and the current month. Add the code from Listing 10-10 and run the query to calculate the prior month value, month-over-month growth and month-over-month growth percentage. The table in Figure 10-10 shows the results.

Listing 10-10. Growth: Comparing the current month to the prior month

```
LAG(SUM(f.SalesAmount), 1, 0)
    OVER(ORDER BY p.CalendarYear, p.CalendarMonth) as [Sales PM],
 -- [Growth] = [CM] - [PM]
    SUM(COALESCE(f.SalesAmount,0))
      - LAG(SUM(f.SalesAmount), 1, 0)
            OVER(ORDER BY p.CalendarYear, p.CalendarMonth)
    AS [MOM Growth],
 -- [Pct Growth] = ([CM] - [PM]) / [PM]
(SUM(COALESCE(f.SalesAmount,0))
  - LAG(SUM(f.SalesAmount), 1, 0)
        OVER(ORDER BY p.CalendarYear, p.CalendarMonth))
    / NULLIF(LAG(SUM(f.SalesAmount), 1, 0 )
            OVER(ORDER BY p.CalendarYear, p.CalendarMonth),0)
    AS [MOM Growth %]
```

	RowID	OrderYear	OrderMonth	Sales Amt	Sales Amt YTD	Sales Amt PM	PM MOM Growth	PM MOM Growth %
1	1	2011	1	469823.91	469823.91	0.00	469823.9148	NULL
2	2	2011	2	466334.90	936158.82	469823.9148	-3489.0118	-0.0074
3	3	2011	3	485198.66	1421357.48	466334.903	18863.7564	0.0404
4	4	2011	4	502073.85	1923431.32	485198.6594	16875.1864	0.0347
5	5	2011	5	561681.48	2485112.80	502073.8458	59607.63	0.1187
6	6	2011	6	737839.82	3222952.62	561681.4758	176158.3456	0.3136
7	7	2011	7	596746.56	3819699.18	737839.8214	-141093.2646	-0.1912
8	8	2011	8	614557.94	4434257.11	596746.5568	17811.3782	0.0298
9	9	2011	9	603083.50	5037340.61	614557.935	-11474.4374	-0.0186
10	10	2011	10	708208.00	5745548.61	603083.4976	105124.5056	0.1743
11	11	2011	11	660545.81	6406094.43	708208.0032	-47662.19	-0.0672
12	12	2011	12	669431.50	7075525.93	660545.8132	8885.6899	0.0134
13	13	2012	1	495364.13	495364.13	669431.5031	-174067.377	-0.26
14	14	2012	2	506994.19	1002358.31	495364.1261	11630.0615	0.0234
15	15	2012	3	373483.01	1375841.32	506994.1876	-133511.1822	-0.2633
16	16	2012	4	400335.61	1776176.93	373483.0054	26852.6091	0.0718

Figure 10-10. *Difference: Comparing the current month to the prior month*

Summary

This chapter covered a lot of ground, building on previously learned concepts to create complex calculations for time-based financial analysis. Some of the calculations were not previously easily accomplished in T-SQL, let alone in a single query. You learned about the need to have a consistent timeline as the backbone of your queries and how to handle gaps in the data. You learned how to create period-to-date, same period prior year, prior year-to-date, ratio to parent, moving averages, and growth and growth percentage calculations.

Next, Chapter 11 will teach you how to leverage these techniques to create even more useful trend calculations.

CHAPTER 11

Time Trend Calculations

In this chapter you will put all the techniques you have learned in the previous chapter to work to create calculations for navigating the timeline to produce the following calculations:

- Moving total (MT)

- Moving average (MA)

- Rate of change (ROC)

- Putting it all together

- Pareto Principle

Moving Totals and Moving Averages

So far, the queries have become more and more complex. They are about to become even more so. To help keep them understandable, you need to think about them conceptually as a layering of operations, one on top of the other, over the data. The early examples were a single query, aggregating over a set of records in a single pass. To introduce a contiguous range of dates to eliminate gaps in the transaction data, a second operation was added by introducing a CTE to do some prework before the main aggregation query. You have already seen this in Listing 10-4 but will be taking it further in this chapter.

In this section of the chapter, you will be adding a third operation by turning the aggregate from the last example into a CTE and aggregating results on top of it. In some cases, the same results can be achieved with one or two operations, but for cases where the nesting of window function is required, the only option is to add another level. One example of this is calculating [Sales PY YTD] at the month level. To create the [Sales YTD] measure, you had to use all the clauses of the window function. There is not a

© Kathi Kellenberger, Clayton Groom, and Ed Pollack 2019
K. Kellenberger et al., *Expert T-SQL Window Functions in SQL Server 2019*,
https://doi.org/10.1007/978-1-4842-5197-3_11

method left to allow you to shift the partition back to the prior year. By first calculating [Sales YTD] in the second operation, you can then use a window function in the third operation to calculate [Sales PY YTD].

Again, a secondary advantage is that the column calculations on any higher-order operations can use the meaningful column names from the lower-order operations to make the calculations easier to understand and the code more compact. Managing the trade-offs of performance and code readability must be considered as well. The following pseudo-code maps out the logic that will be implemented in T-SQL for the remaining calculations:

```
[Current Sales] = SUM of SalesAmount for a time period (day, month, year)
[Prior Sales] = SUM of SalesAmount for the prior time period
[Growth] = [Current Sales] - [Prior Sales]
[Growth %] = [Growth] / [Prior Sales]
[3 MMT] = Sum of SalesAmount for the prior three months
[12 MMT] = Sum of SalesAmount for the prior 12 months
[3 MMA] = Average of Monthly Sales for the prior three months
[12 MMA] = Average of Monthly Sales for the prior 12 months
[3/12 ROC] = [3 MMT]/([3 MMT].LAG( 11 months))
[12/12 ROC] = [12 MMT] /([12 MMT].LAG( 11 months))
[3/12 RoC2]= ([3 MMT]/([3 MMT].LAG( 11 months))* 100) -100
[12/12 RoC2] = ([12 MMT] /([12 MMT].LAG( 11 months))* 100) -100
```

Ensuring Sets Are Complete

The last item that needs to be addressed is making sure the sets for any moving total or moving average calculation contain the correct number of input rows. For example, a three-month moving average [3 MMA] must contain data from three complete months, or it is not correct. By addressing gaps in transaction date ranges, part of the problem was solved but not the complete problem. At the beginning of a set, the first row has no prior rows, so it is incorrect to calculate a moving average for that row. The second row of the set only has one preceding row, making it incorrect to calculate the average for it as well. Only when the third row is reached are the conditions correct for calculating the three-month moving average. Table 11-1 shows how a three-month average should be calculated, given the prior year had no data for the product:

Table 11-1. *Eliminating incomplete results for averages over ranges of periods*

Month	Product	Sales	Sales YTD	Sales 3 MMA
January	Bacon	1000	1000	
February	Bacon	500	1500	
March	Bacon	1500	3000	1000
April	Bacon	600	3600	867
May	Bacon	0	3600	700
June	Bacon	400	4000	333

To make this work, you simply COUNT the number of rows in the frame for the three-month period instead of averaging the results and use the count to determine when to perform the calculation. If there are three rows, perform the calculation; otherwise return a null value. The following example uses a CASE statement to determine which rows have two preceding rows:

```
CASE WHEN COUNT(*)
          OVER (ORDER BY p.CalendarYear, p.CalendarMonth
          ROWS BETWEEN 2 PRECEDING AND CURRENT ROW) = 3
             THEN AVG(SUM(f.SalesAmount))
          OVER(ORDER BY p.CalendarYear, p.CalendarMonth
          ROWS BETWEEN 2 PRECEDING AND current row)
             ELSE null
     END AS [Sales 3 MMA]
```

The query in Listing 11-1 includes moving total and moving average calculations for 3-month and 12-month rolling periods. These are implemented in the second CTE operation, so that the results are available for further manipulation in the third operations select statement.

Listing 11-1. Updated Base Query Using CTE

```
/* 11.1 Month level, no product. Handling gaps, All products, 3 operation
query */
WITH CTE_ProductPeriod /* Operation #1 Generate the product period
framework */
AS  (
    SELECT p.ProductKey, Datekey,
            CalendarYear, CalendarQuarter,
            MonthNumberOfYear AS CalendarMonth
    FROM DimDate AS d
    CROSS JOIN DimProduct p
    WHERE d.FullDateAlternateKey BETWEEN '2011-01-01' AND GETDATE()
    AND EXISTS(SELECT * FROM FactInternetSales f
                WHERE f.ProductKey = p.ProductKey
                AND f.OrderDate BETWEEN '2011-01-01' AND GETDATE())
        ),
CTE_MonthlySummary /* Operation #2 Calculate the base statistics */
AS (
    SELECT ROW_NUMBER()
            OVER(ORDER BY p.CalendarYear, p.CalendarMonth) AS [RowID],
        p.CalendarYear AS OrderYear,
        p.CalendarMonth AS OrderMonth,
        count(distinct f.SalesOrderNumber) AS [Order Count],
        count(distinct f.CustomerKey) AS [Customer Count],
        ROUND(SUM(COALESCE(f.SalesAmount,0)), 2) AS [Sales],
        ROUND(SUM(SUM(COALESCE(f.SalesAmount, 0)))
                OVER(PARTITION BY p.CalendarYear
                    ORDER BY p.CalendarYear, p.CalendarMonth
                    ROWS BETWEEN UNBOUNDED PRECEDING AND CURRENT ROW
                    ), 2)
            AS [Sales YTD],
        ROUND(LAG(SUM(f.SalesAmount), 11, 0 )
                OVER(ORDER BY p.CalendarYear, p.CalendarMonth), 2)
            AS [Sales SP PY],
```

```
       ROUND(LAG(SUM(f.SalesAmount), 1, 0)
              OVER(ORDER BY p.CalendarYear, p.CalendarMonth), 2)
          AS [Sales PM],
       CASE WHEN COUNT(*)
              OVER(ORDER BY p.CalendarYear, p.CalendarMonth
                  ROWS BETWEEN 2 PRECEDING AND CURRENT ROW) = 3
          THEN AVG(SUM(f.SalesAmount))
              OVER(ORDER BY p.CalendarYear, p.CalendarMonth
                  ROWS BETWEEN 2 PRECEDING AND current row)
          ELSE null
       END AS [Sales 3 MMA],  /* 3 Month Moving Average */
       CASE WHEN count(*)
              OVER(ORDER BY p.CalendarYear, p.CalendarMonth
                  ROWS BETWEEN 2 PRECEDING AND current row) = 3
          THEN SUM(SUM(f.SalesAmount))
              OVER(ORDER BY p.CalendarYear, p.CalendarMonth
                  ROWS BETWEEN 2 PRECEDING AND current row)
             ELSE null
       END AS [Sales 3 MMT],   /* 3 month Moving Total */
       CASE WHEN COUNT(*)
              OVER (ORDER BY p.CalendarYear, p.CalendarMonth
                  ROWS BETWEEN 11 PRECEDING AND CURRENT ROW) = 12
          THEN AVG(SUM(f.SalesAmount))
              OVER(ORDER BY p.CalendarYear, p.CalendarMonth
                  ROWS BETWEEN 11 PRECEDING AND current row)
          ELSE null
       END AS [Sales 12 MMA], /* 12 Month Moving Average */
       CASE WHEN count(*)
              OVER(ORDER BY p.CalendarYear, p.CalendarMonth
             ROWS BETWEEN 11 PRECEDING AND current row) = 12
       THEN SUM(SUM(f.SalesAmount))
             OVER (ORDER BY p.CalendarYear, p.CalendarMonth
                  ROWS BETWEEN 11 PRECEDING AND current row)
       ELSE null
     END AS [Sales 12 MMT]  /* 12 month Moving Total */
FROM CTE_ProductPeriod AS p
```

```
LEFT OUTER JOIN [dbo].[FactInternetSales] AS f
    ON p.ProductKey = f.ProductKey
    AND p.DateKey = f.OrderDateKey
GROUP BY p.CalendarYear, p.CalendarMonth
)
SELECT [RowID],
    [OrderYear],
    [OrderMonth],
    [Order Count],
    [Customer Count],
    [Sales],
    [Sales SP PY],
    [Sales PM],
    [Sales YTD],
    [Sales 3 MMA],
    [Sales 3 MMT],
    [Sales 12 MMA],
    [Sales 12 MMT],
    [Sales] - [Sales SP PY] AS [Sales SP PY Growth],
    ([Sales] - [Sales SP PY])
        / NULLIF([Sales SP PY], 0) AS [Sales SP PY Growth %],
    [Sales] - [Sales SP PY] AS [Sales PY MOM Growth],
    ([Sales] - [Sales PM])
        / NULLIF([Sales PM], 0) AS [Sales PY MOM Growth %]
FROM CTE_MonthlySummary
ORDER BY [OrderYear], [OrderMonth]
```

Notice how much simpler and readable the final select is. Because you encapsulated the logic behind the columns in the previous CTE operation, the resulting columns are also available to be used in operation, including window functions!

The addition of the Moving Monthly Totals (MMT) and Moving Monthly Average (MMA) that were added to the summary provides a way to address seasonality in the data by averaging the monthly totals across a range of months. Moving totals and averages are useful because they smooth out the volatility in seasonal/noisy data. They can also be used to calculate an annual rate of change (RoC) which can be used to identify trends and measure cyclical change over longer periods of time.

You could not create a column for [Sales YTD PY] until now. With the [Sales YTD] column present in every row of the CTE, you can now use a window function to look back to the same period in the prior year and use it to calculate a difference between the current year to date and the prior year to date. Remember, even though you are working with a query that returns data at a month level, this technique works for date level results as well. Add the following block of column calculations in Listing 11-2 to the new base query from Listing 11-1 and explore the results.

Listing 11-2. Same Period Prior Year-to-Date Calculations

```
LAG([Sales YTD], 11,0)
    OVER(ORDER BY [OrderYear], [OrderMonth])
    AS [Sales PY YTD],
[Sales YTD] - LAG([Sales YTD], 11,0)
                    OVER(ORDER BY [OrderYear], [OrderMonth])
    AS [Sales PY YTD Diff],
([Sales YTD] - LAG([Sales YTD], 11,0)
                    OVER(ORDER BY [OrderYear], [OrderMonth]))
        /NULLIF(LAG([Sales YTD], 11, 0)
                    OVER(ORDER BY [OrderYear], [OrderMonth]), 0)
    AS [Sales PY YTD Pct Diff]
```

Because of the number of columns returned in this query, the chart in Figure 11-1 makes more sense to demonstrate the results. The whole purpose of creating the growth and growth percent calculations is to be able to use them to analyze the data for trends. Plotting the data in a chart is a great way to visualize the results and present them to business users.

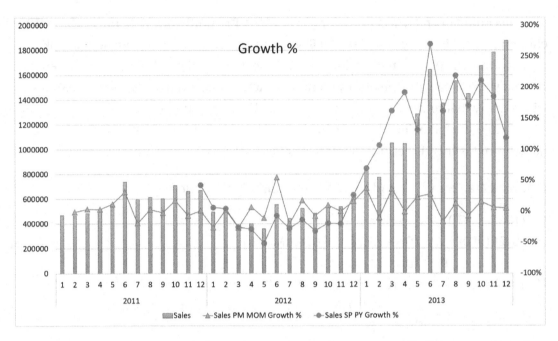

Figure 11-1. *Monthly trend chart showing month-over-month difference % and same period PY difference %*

Month-over-month (MOM) difference calculations are generally not that useful as a direct measure. They show the change from one period to the next, which can be very "noisy" and can hide underlying trends. Same period prior year (SP PY) difference calculations show a better picture of the growth trend over the prior year, but can also be prone to seasonality. Big changes in sales can often be attributed to the holiday season, and do not always reflect the overall trends at work. That being said, you are now going to improve upon these calculations by implementing the rate-of-change calculations mentioned previously and smooth out the seasonal ups and downs into long-term trends.

Rate of Change

Rates of change are the percentage of change in a moving total or moving average and indicate if a measure is improving over the prior year or getting worse. They are useful for determining leading and lagging indicators between divergent information sources. Leading indicators are things that can be used to predict forces of change for a business. For example, if your business relies on petrochemical feedstocks to produce its products, changes to oil prices are likely to presage a change in demand for your products and could be considered a leading indicator. Charting the rate of change for corporate sales alongside the rate of change for stock market and commodity indices allows you to determine if your company's performance leads, lags, or is coincident with the performance of the stock market.

Add the following block of column calculations in Listing 11-3 to the query from Listing 11-2 and explore the results.

Listing 11-3. Rate of Change Calculations

```
/* Rate of Change [3 MMT]/([3 MMT].LAG( 12 months)) */
[Sales 3 MMT]
   / LAG(NULLIF([Sales 3 MMT], 0), 11, null)
        OVER(ORDER BY [OrderYear], [OrderMonth])
   as [3/12 RoC],
/* [12 MMT] /([12 MMT].LAG( 12 months)) */
[Sales 12 MMT]
   / LAG(NULLIF([Sales 12 MMT],0), 11, null)
        OVER(ORDER BY [OrderYear], [OrderMonth])
   as [12/12 RoC]
```

Rate of change less than 1.0 (100%) are downward trends and rates of change 1.0 or greater are positive change. The calculation can also be amended to turn the ratio into a positive or negative number as follows:

```
/* Rate of Change +/- ([3 MMT]/([3 MMT].LAG( 12 months))* 100) -100 */
([Sales 3 MMT] / LAG(NULLIF([Sales 3 MMT], 0), 11, null)
   OVER(ORDER BY [OrderYear], [OrderMonth]) *100) - 100
   as [3/12 RoC2],
/* ([12 MMT] /([12 MMT].LAG( 12 months))* 100) -100 */
   ([Sales 12 MMT] / LAG(NULLIF([Sales 12 MMT],0), 11, null)
   OVER(ORDER BY [OrderYear], [OrderMonth]) *100) - 100
   as [12/12 RoC2]
```

The results of the rate-of-change calculations are best visualized in a chart. In comparison to the chart for the difference percentages, you should notice a closer correlation of the [RoC] measures to the natural curve of the total. The [RoC] measure in this example is a lagging indicator of sales, because it is based on sales. Comparing multiple [ROC] series from different source measures can lead to discovering Leading indicators for key metrics in your business. The second form of the [ROC] calculation is used in Figure 11-2. Note that for most of the 2012 year, the rate of change was negative, despite sales appearing to be relatively flat from month to month for the year.

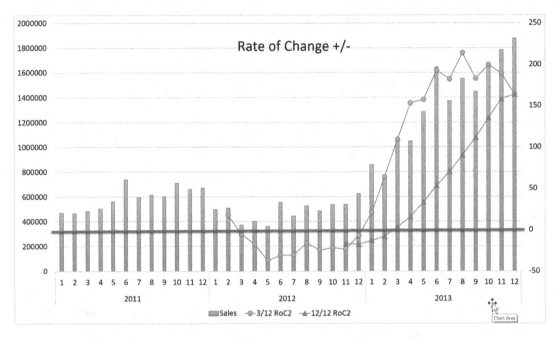

Figure 11-2. *Rate of change trends for 3- and 12-month ranges*

Pareto Principle

The Pareto Principle, named after the Italian economist Vilfredo Pareto, is commonly known as the 80/20 rule. It states that roughly 80% of the effects come from 20% of the causes.[1] Applying the principle can help us identify the most important areas to focus on in our business. For example, determining the top 20% of products by sales can feed into other types of analysis and decision-making.

The calculation for a Pareto analysis/charts is done by ordering the items to be evaluated by the amount being analyzed and calculating a cumulative or rolling sum per item. The cumulative sum is then divided by the overall total to determine a percentage.

---

[1]https://en.wikipedia.org/wiki/Pareto_principle

The pseudo-code would be:

```
[All Sales] = SUM([SalesAmount])
[Cumulative Sales] = cumulative SUM([SalesAmount])
[PARETO] = [Cumulative Sales] / [All Sales]
```

In the case of our sample data, the Pareto Principle, as implemented in Listing 11-4 and shown in Figure 11-3, will help us determine the products that produce the majority of revenue.

Listing 11-4. Pareto Principle

```
SELECT ps.EnglishProductSubcategoryName AS [Sub Category],
       SUM(f.SalesAmount) AS [Sub Category Sales],
       SUM(SUM(f.SalesAmount)) OVER ()        AS [All Sales],
       SUM(SUM(f.SalesAmount)) OVER (ORDER BY SUM(f.SalesAmount) DESC)
       AS [Cumulative Sales],
       SUM(SUM(f.SalesAmount)) OVER (ORDER BY SUM(f.SalesAmount) DESC)
             / SUM(SUM(f.SalesAmount)) OVER () AS [Sales Pareto]
FROM dbo.FactInternetSales AS f
INNER JOIN dbo.DimProduct AS p
       ON f.ProductKey = p.ProductKey
       INNER JOIN dbo.DimProductSubcategory AS ps
             ON p.ProductSubcategoryKey = ps.ProductSubcategoryKey
WHERE OrderDate BETWEEN '2011-01-01' AND '2012-12-31'
GROUP BY ps.ProductSubCategoryKey,
       ps.EnglishProductSubcategoryName
order by [Sales Pareto]
```

	Sub Category	Sub Category Sales	All Sales	Cumulative Sales	Sales Pareto
1	Road Bikes	9298045.0499	12918011.1243	9298045.0499	0.7197
2	Mountain Bikes	3595785.3344	12918011.1243	12893830.3843	0.9981
3	Touring Bikes	21390.87	12918011.1243	12915221.2543	0.9997
4	Helmets	909.74	12918011.1243	12916130.9943	0.9998
5	Tires and Tubes	577.84	12918011.1243	12916708.8343	0.9998
6	Jerseys	415.92	12918011.1243	12917124.7543	0.9999
7	Bottles and Cages	280.62	12918011.1243	12917405.3743	0.9999
8	Bike Stands	159.00	12918011.1243	12917564.3743	0.9999
9	Hydration Packs	109.98	12918011.1243	12917674.3543	0.9999
10	Fenders	109.90	12918011.1243	12917784.2543	0.9999
11	Gloves	73.47	12918011.1243	12917857.7243	0.9999
12	Caps	71.92	12918011.1243	12917929.6443	0.9999
13	Vests	63.50	12918011.1243	12917993.1443	0.9999
14	Socks	17.98	12918011.1243	12918011.1243	1.00

Figure 11-3. *Pareto calculation over all subcategories*

This example shows all the pieces involved in determining the [Sales Pareto] column, but because so much of the sales volume consists of road bikes, we'll need to dig into that subcategory to demonstrate a more typical Pareto result. In Listing 11-5, the [All Sales] and [Cumulative Sales] columns can be removed as they are only needed for the [Sales Pareto] calculation itself. Adding in a sum of quantity gives more context to the results, as seen in Figure 11-4.

Listing 11-5. Pareto Refined

```
SELECT p.EnglishProductName as [Product],
       SUM(f.SalesAmount) AS [Sub Category Sales],
       SUM(f.OrderQuantity) AS [Sub Category Qty],
       SUM(SUM(f.SalesAmount)) OVER (ORDER BY SUM(f.SalesAmount) DESC)
             / SUM(SUM(f.SalesAmount)) OVER () AS [Sales Pareto]
FROM dbo.FactInternetSales AS f
INNER JOIN dbo.DimProduct AS p
       ON f.ProductKey = p.ProductKey
       INNER JOIN dbo.DimProductSubcategory AS ps
             ON p.ProductSubcategoryKey = ps.ProductSubcategoryKey
WHERE OrderDate BETWEEN '2011-01-01' AND '2012-12-31'
and ps.EnglishProductSubcategoryName = 'Road Bikes'
```

```
GROUP BY P.EnglishProductName
,ps.ProductSubCategoryKey,
        ps.EnglishProductSubcategoryName
order by [Sales Pareto]
```

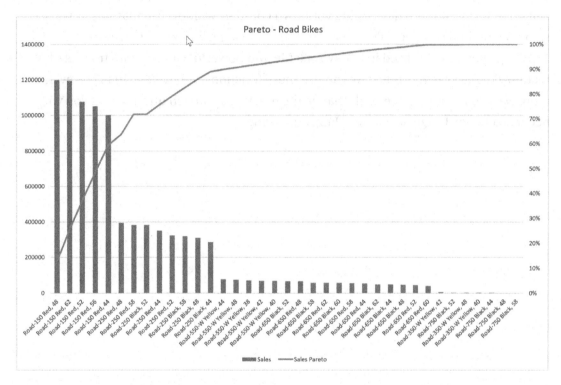

Figure 11-4. *Road bike sales Pareto by product*

Adding a Pareto column to an existing report query is now a high-value, low-effort exercise thanks to the power of window functions!

Summary

This chapter covered a lot of ground, building on previously learned concepts to create complex trending calculations for time-based financial analysis. The approach of creating and validating input calculations before tackling more complex calculations will serve you well when developing your own complex window calculations as will the stepwise method of using CTEs to get around the nesting limitation of window functions.

I hope you have realized just how versatile and powerful window functions are by reading the pages of this book. As you use these functions, you will begin to see even more ways to use them. They will change the way you approach queries, and you will become a better T-SQL developer. Happy querying!

Index

© Kathi Kellenberger, Clayton Groom, and Ed Pollack 2019
K. Kellenberger et al., *Expert T-SQL Window Functions in SQL Server 2019*,
https://doi.org/10.1007/978-1-4842-5197-3

Y, Z

Printed in the United States
By Bookmasters